All-Time Greats of
BOXING

All-Time Greats of
BOXING

Peter Arnold

Foreword by Henry Cooper

MAGNA BOOKS

Published by Magna Books
Magna Road
Wigston
Leicester LE8 2XH

Produced by Bison Books Ltd
176 Old Brompton Road
London SW5 0BA
England

ISBN 0 948509 65 1

Printed in Hong Kong

Reprinted 1988

Photographs
Page 1: Muhammad Ali.
Page 2: Sugar Ray Leonard (*top*); Larry Holmes (*bottom left*);
Barry McGuigan (*bottom right*).
Page 3: Marvin Hagler (*left*); Thomas Hearns (*right*).
This page: Thomas Hearns (facing) and Mark Medal.
Page 5: Don Curry (*right*) and Colin Jones (*left*).

Contents

Foreword

by Henry Cooper

Boxing as we know it now has been going on for over 100 years, since the Marquess of Queensberry published his famous rules in 1867. One of the most important of these was the introduction of gloves, bringing to an end the days of bare-knuckle prize fighting.

The last of the bare-knuckle heavyweight champions was John L Sullivan, who also took part in the first heavyweight title bout in which the boxers wore gloves. It is with his story that this book begins.

Of the 39 champions from those 100 years whose careers are outlined, 16 are heavyweights, my own weight class, and I suppose it's the heavyweights who most capture the imagination of the public. After all, there's an old saying in the fight game that boxing is as good as the heavyweight champion. Since Ali there have been two and at the start of 1987 even three men claiming to be heavyweight champion of the world.

At present there is a plan afoot to unify the heavyweight championship, and some time in 1987, if all goes well, there will be only one champion again. If the same thing could be achieved through all the weight divisions, it would be the best thing to happen to boxing for a long time. Of the men whose stories are included here and who are still fighting today, only Marvin Hagler in the middleweights is currently a true world champion – it would give the fight game more appeal if there were a genuine world champ at every weight.

Boxing needs everything it can get to help it, because there is always a body of opinion knocking it and trying to ban it on the grounds that it does a lot of harm to boxers. I can only speak for myself, and it has done me nothing but good. I thoroughly enjoyed all my years in the ring, although there was plenty I had to go without to get to the top. That needs dedication and early nights. Since I hung up my gloves (or, to be more exact, gave them away for charity) I've enjoyed just as much what boxing has brought me: a nice home, going places and meeting people that I would not have met otherwise. And let's be honest, it's good to be recognized, too, especially as people on the whole are kind enough to respect your privacy, and don't come up and ask for an autograph while you're having a meal in a restaurant.

I myself was lucky enough to come from a good home and a close family, but as you read these stories of the great champions, you will realize the sort of life many of them might have led without boxing. There has never been too much chance for really poor boys from places like Mexico City or the East Side of New York to become rich and world-famous. Statistics would show, I expect, that there was more chance that they would become criminals. The most important day in the lives of many of the men featured in these pages was the day somebody took them off the streets, pointed them in the direction of a gym and first fitted them up with boxing gloves.

Nowadays a golf glove is more familiar to me, and I get most of my sporting pleasure trying to knock that infuriating little white ball in the direction of the flag. It's the left hand that does most of the work, as usual. But I keep well in touch with the fight game at all levels from boys up. Most fight people are my friends, especially those who do the business at the sharp end – the men and boys who climb into the ring and lead with their chins, as we say. I've got the greatest respect for all fighters. Some of the best there have ever been feature in this book. I hope you enjoy finding out about them from the comfortable side of the ropes.

Left: Henry Cooper, one of the all-time greats of British boxing, remains much in demand on the celebrity circuit. (Fabergé)
Right: The younger Cooper training in the famous gym at the Thomas a'Becket public house in the Old Kent Road. He was British heavyweight champion for over ten years. (TPS/CLI)

Introduction

Above: Jack Johnson, the first black heavyweight champion of the world, a great boxer who caused much controversy.

Boxing is the most primitive of sports. This is part of its appeal, as it rewards basic qualities such as strength and courage, which are easily discerned and universally admired by spectators. But it also brings a threat. Boxing, according to its critics, is the only sport in which participants deliberately set out to cause harm to each other. According to most medical opinion they succeed too well, the harm often being permanent. So boxing has, on the one hand, a strong medical lobby trying to stop it, and, on the other, such a worldwide following wanting to see the best practitioners that Sugar Ray Leonard can earn $11 million for less than an hour's work.

If the doctors succeed, they could end 300 years of the second period of recorded boxing history. The first period begins with Egyptian hieroglyphics from around 4000 BC. Homer in the *Iliad* and Virgil in the *Aeneid* mention boxing. Boxing was introduced into the ancient Olympic Games in 688 BC. The boxers, then as now, were heroes commemorated by writers and sculptors and worshiped by their local supporters. It was the influence of the Romans, with their liking for gladiatorial combat, which hastened the end of the first period of boxing history. They introduced studs into the primitive boxing glove, called a *cestus*, causing losers to be beaten to near-death. The banning of the *cestus*, followed by the termination of the Olympic Games by Theodosius the Great in 393 AD, led to the virtual disappearance of boxing as a spectator sport for around 1300 years.

The English, who invented many of the world's current sports, re-invented boxing toward the end of the seventeenth century, giving it its second period of popularity. As fist-fighting was seen to attract spectators, men good at it began to tour the country, challenging locals, often at fairs. Spectators would form a circle round the combatants by holding a length of rope. Hence the 'ring', which is today square. The first report of a boxing match from this period appeared in the *Protestant Mercury* in January 1681. Teachers of fencing and the use of the quarterstaff began also to teach boxing, which was included in the 'noble science of defence'. One of these, James Figg, was claimed by a client, Captain Godfrey, to be the champion of England, virtually, in fact, the champion of the world. Since Figg, hundreds of men have been acknowledged as champions.

This book describes the careers of 39 of the greatest of them. The first, chronologically, is John L Sullivan, the last bare-knuckle champion. His career straddled two eras. The bare-knuckle era had been governed by rules since 1743, when champion Jack Broughton, having so beaten a challenger that he died, published a set of rules designed to reduce the chances of such tragedies. Nearly 100 years later, these rules were refined, becoming the London Prize Ring Rules, but a much bigger change came in 1867, when the Marquess of Queensberry published his rules. The Queensberry Rules, which specified the wearing of gloves and the three-minute round, form the basis of the rules used today. John L Sullivan, the bare-knuckle champion, defended his title wearing gloves, in what has come to be regarded as the first fight for the heavyweight championship of the world.

The heavyweights have always commanded most interest among the fans, and consequently 16 of the boxers included in this book are from that class. Some picked themselves – Jack Johnson, the great black boxer who so infuriated the white race; Jack Dempsey, one of the best at the box-office, whose exciting fights drew the first five million-dollar gates; Joe Louis, who made more successful title defenses than any other boxer; Rocky Marciano, the only unbeaten heavyweight champion; and Muhammad Ali, whose career was perhaps the most extraordinary of all. Each of these men would have supporters as the greatest of all time.

Other heavyweights whose careers are included are

Gene Tunney, the conqueror of Dempsey; Max Schmeling, who knocked out Louis; Jersey Joe Walcott, the oldest of all; Floyd Patterson, the first to regain the title; Ingemar Johansson, the most surprising; Sonny Liston, the most menacing; Henry Cooper, who almost knocked out Ali; Joe Frazier, who fought Ali three times, winning once: Larry Holmes, who nearly equalled Marciano's unbeaten record; and Mike Tyson, the youngest champion.

Georges Carpentier, the amazing French 'Orchid Man,' and Michael Spinks, who won the IBF version of the heavyweight title, are included to represent the light-heavyweights.

There are eight middleweights included. This division has always been one of the most competitive, and it has produced some of the greatest champions of all. Indeed, the excellence of middleweight boxing makes one wonder if there is something special about the 160-pound weight limit. Is this perhaps man's ideal weight?

The eight, all of whom fought after the Second World War, are Tony Zale, the 'Man of Steel'; Rocky Graziano, perhaps the best of the rags-to-riches stories; Marcel Cerdan, the great Frenchman, killed in his prime; Jake LaMotta, subject of an excellent feature film; Sugar Ray Robinson, perhaps the best; Randolph Turpin, who beat him; Carlos Monzon, who retired undefeated; and Marvelous Marvin Hagler, who still reigns.

There have been some excellent welterweights in the 1970s and 1980s. To represent days past in this division are Ted Kid Lewis, who held nine national and international titles, a record, and Henry Armstrong, the only boxer to hold three world titles simultaneously. Three moderns make up the number: Thomas Hearns, the 'Hit Man', one of today's most exciting performers; Sugar Ray Leonard, the classiest boxer of recent times; Don Curry, the undisputed champion of the mid 1980s.

Two modern lightweights represent their class: Roberto Duran, the macho man, who has fought the best in the world from light to middleweight, and held his own, and Alexis Arguello, who similarly took on the best at four weights. There are two featherweights: Sandy Saddler, whose fights with Willie Pep are notorious, and Barry McGuigan, who excited all Ireland and Britain with his skills. Ruben Olivares is chosen to represent the bantam class – few men of his weight have ever punched as hard as Olivares.

The flyweights are represented by the first world champion, and, many would say, still the best, Jimmy Wilde; Benny Lynch, who destroyed himself, in the style of classic tragedy; and Pascual Perez, a modern version of Wilde, a tiny man with a tremendous punch.

The main feeling of one who has chosen a selection of men to represent the great champions is, of course, guilt and regret at the ones left out. Bob Fitzsimmons, for example, the Cornishman who won the middle, light-heavy and heavyweight titles, or Jim Jeffries, who took his heavyweight crown. And all those brilliant middleweights up to the Second World War: Jack Dempsey, called 'The Nonpareil' because he had no equal; Stanley Ketchel, assassinated in his prime by a jealous cowhand; Harry Greb, the only man to beat Tunney; and Mickey Walker, who fought Greb twice in one evening, the second time outside a New York night-club where both

Above: Muhammad Ali, another boxer whose long career was marked by controversy, including a dispute with the US Army.

had taken their post-fight parties. And then there is the lightweight Benny Leonard, and the prince of featherweights, 'Peerless' Jim Driscoll.

In the battle for limited space, the more recent boxers have tended to get the referee's nod.

In current professional boxing, there are more weight divisions than the 'classic' eight mentioned above. In-between weights have gradually been added, and given various names. Thus the weight between flyweight and bantam is variously called light-bantam (the description favored in this book), junior bantam, or super-fly. There are now 15 classes recognized by various bodies. The poundage range within each class has, of course, narrowed, and many boxers campaign equally well in two, or even three, classes.

There are also three bodies, the International Boxing Federation, the World Boxing Association and the World Boxing Council, who recognize world champions. This means that instead of the eight world champions of the early 1950s, there are now usually more than 30. This, of course, very much devalues the title of 'world champion'. Toward the end of 1986 there were only two boxers who could truly be called world champions, the undisputed middle and welterweight title holders, Marvin Hagler and Lloyd Honeyghan.

The best thing that could happen to boxing is that the ruling bodies could come to an agreement on one champion for each weight. A start has been made to unify the heavyweight division. When all world champions really are world champions, the big fights will be genuine big fights again, and not just television ratings weapons.

Meanwhile the great boxers can still excite worldwide audiences, and the stories of 39 of the best are told in the following pages.

Heavyweight

Floyd Patterson (right) scattering the perspiration of Tommy 'Hurricane' Jackson in Patterson's first defense of the title in 1957.

John L Sullivan
Bare-knuckles and booze

John L Sullivan was a larger-than-life character, a handsome mustachioed man who did not allow training to interfere with his love of the good life, especially where a pretty girl and a strong drink were concerned. He would enter a saloon and boast that he could lick any mother's son in the house. He became a legend in America, so that any fan who had met him would invite others to 'shake the hand of a man who shook the hand of John L Sullivan.'

Sullivan was born in Roxburg, Massachusetts, on 15 October 1858. He grew to 5 feet 10½ inches and 196 pounds, and his strength enabled him, it was said, to lift a derailed streetcar back onto the rails. He liked scrapping and his followers called him the Boston Strong Boy. He won many bare-knuckle fights and claimed the title of heavyweight champion of America by knocking out Paddy Ryan from Tipperary in 1882. Ryan was a protégé of Richard K Fox, the publisher of the *New York Police Gazette*, a theatrical and sporting weekly which helped shape the boxing opinion of the time. Sullivan snubbed Fox and made an influential enemy.

Another enemy who was to figure in Sullivan's subsequent career was Charlie Mitchell, a clever English fighter from Birmingham, who was not much more than a middleweight, but who challenged Sullivan to a three-round bout at Madison Square Garden, New York, and had the cheek to outbox him and put him on the floor with a right to the chin. The enraged Sullivan had Mitchell in trouble in the third, but could not finish the job and nurtured a hatred for the cocky limey.

In 1887 Sullivan went to London and boxed an exhibition for the Prince of Wales (later Edward VII). He challenged the British champion Jem Smith, but Smith was preparing for a bout with Jake Kilrain. Little Charlie Mitchell was on hand, however, claiming Sullivan was frightened of him and taunting him to such effect that John L agreed to fight him for a £500 side-stake. Because prize-fighting was then illegal in England a match was arranged to take place in secret on the gallops of Baron Rothschild's racing stables at Chantilly, France, on 10 March 1888.

Below left: John L Sullivan plants a right onto the chin of the man who tormented him more than once, the English middleweight Charlie Mitchell, in their 1888 battle at Baron Rothschild's racing stables in France.
Below center: The young John L Sullivan, the 'Boston Strong Boy,' the 'Champion of Champions,' and the last of the bare-knuckle champions, displaying his fine shoulders and biceps.
Below right: John L Sullivan, without his mustache in 1885.

Less than 50 spectators saw the fight, held in bitterly cold rain. Sullivan was 35 pounds heavier and began as if he were going to knock Mitchell's head off, but Mitchell danced through the mud, Sullivan tired, and after 39 rounds and over three hours the Englishman was getting on top when the police were spotted. Somebody called it a draw, before both badly battered men were arrested for breaking the law and fined.

Meanwhile Jake Kilrain, from Quincy, Massachusetts, had drawn his fight with Jem Smith, also in France, hostilities being stopped because of darkness after 106 ferocious rounds. Kilrain, like Sullivan of Irish descent, was also unbeaten after nine years' campaigning. Richard K Fox thought Jake could beat Sullivan and issued a challenge on his behalf. Sullivan, preferring the easy life, declined, at which Fox publicly presented Kilrain with a magnificent belt and proclaimed him Champion of America by default.

Sullivan's Boston fans immediately clubbed together for a grander belt, 12 inches wide, with gold panels and 397 diamonds spelling his name, which had 'Champion of Champions' above it. A proud John L publicly proclaimed the *Police Gazette* belt a dog-collar.

The challenge of Kilrain could not be ignored forever, though, and on 8 July 1889 John L fought him at Richburg, Mississippi. The purse was $10,000, winner take all. Because of his liking for soft living Sullivan would have had little chance but for William Muldoon, a wrestler and physical culture fanatic. He was engaged to get the flabby Sullivan fit.

It was a hard battle with little attention paid to rules, fought in heat which seemed to affect Kilrain more. After

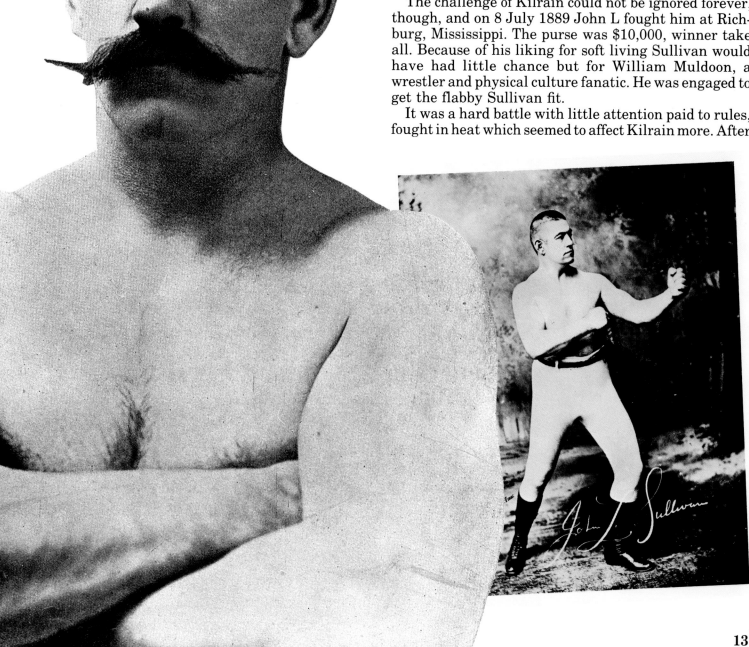

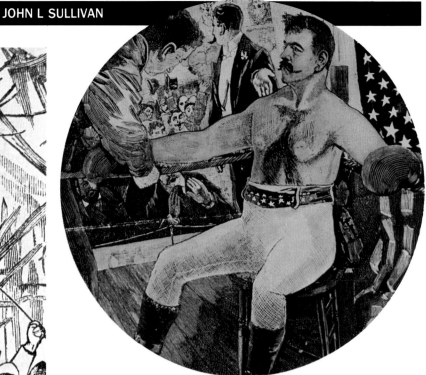

Above: John L Sullivan, probably during one of his theatrical performances before he met Corbett for the championship.
Left: Sullivan (left) beating Kilrain in Richmond, Mississippi, in the last bare-knuckle championship fight on 8 July 1889.

over two hours and 75 rounds Kilrain's corner (in which was the ubiquitous Mitchell) was told by a doctor that any more punishment could lead to Jake's death, and so the towel was thrown in. Fox's belt went with the championship but Sullivan tossed it to a handler as a collar for his dog.

The fight drew widespread publicity and Sullivan, now claiming to be champion of the world, cashed in by touring in a melodrama entitled 'Honest Hearts and Willing Hands.' Theaters were packed to see the great man, who resumed his life of champagne-quaffing ease. He had a paunch when challenged for his crown by James J Corbett in 1892.

By now the Queensberry Rules, which specified the use of gloves, were gaining acceptance. The Kilrain fight was the last big bare-knuckle fight in America. The match between Corbett and Sullivan is thus acknowledged as the first for the heavyweight championship of the world. It was a match of contrasts: Sullivan the old bare-knuckle roisterer versus Corbett, eight years his junior, an immaculate dresser who earned his nickname Gentleman Jim. Corbett was an ex-bank clerk, keen on physical culture, a man trained in the science of boxing by an English instructor.

The match was on 7 September 1892 at New Orleans. The stylish Corbett outboxed the heavier Sullivan, toyed with him like a matador with a bull, and knocked him out in the twenty-first round. The crowd did not like the new style of defensive boxing, and booed. It was truly the end of an era. The old braggart, Sullivan, made a generous speech and left weeping, more loved than ever in defeat, to become a national institution.

John L did not challenge again. He reformed. He became an evangelist, and married his childhood sweetheart. Together they toured the States preaching against drink until he died on 2 February 1918.

Jack Johnson
Women were his downfall

Jack Johnson was the most hated of all boxers. He fought at a time when white boxers could 'draw the color line' and avoid facing a black man. Black boxers could only get contests with each other. Occasionally several black fighters would be put into a ring together to fight until only one winner was left. These were called 'battle royals.' It was from this harsh environment that Johnson eventually proved himself the best in the world.

John Arthur Johnson was born in Galveston, Texas, on 31 March 1878. He boxed professionally from his teens, and by the time he was 30 had beaten all the best black boxers and those white ones willing to fight him, including ex-world champion Bob Fitzsimmons. The reigning champion was Tommy Burns, a Canadian, who cashed in by going on a world tour, beating opponents in London and Paris. Thinking he might get a shot at the title abroad, Johnson followed him, and in Australia got his chance to fight Burns for the championship.

A caterer called Hugh D (Huge Deal) McIntosh put up

Above: Johnson, facing camera, on his way to the heavyweight title in Australia in 1908, against Tommy Burns of Canada.

£6000 which persuaded Burns to accept the challenge. McIntosh built a ring at Rushcutters' Bay, Sydney, and put on the much-publicized black versus white showdown on Boxing Day, 1908. Sixteen thousand fans paid £26,000 to see the fight, and McIntosh made a fortune (many years later he opened a Black and White chain of milk bars which enjoyed a vogue in London).

Johnson was a master of defensive boxing and at 6 feet 1 inch and some 200 pounds enjoyed huge physical advantages over Burns, who at 5 feet 7 inches was the shortest of all heavyweight champions. Johnson played with Burns, all the frustrations of years of being kept in his place coming to the fore. He insulted the champion, smiled at his efforts, and battered him at will until a police inspector stopped the carnage in the fourteenth.

Jack London, the famous writer, was at the ringside, and said that the arrogant smile must be wiped from the new champion's face, and all white America agreed. The tough middleweight champion Stanley Ketchel, the 'Michigan Assassin,' tried at Colma in October 1909. It was a mismatch and the fight was probably fixed, but all collusion ended in the twelfth round when Stanley threw a right and dumped Johnson on his trunks. Johnson, feeling double-crossed, got up with murder in his heart, and as Ketchel leapt in rashly for the supposed kill hit him with an uppercut to the mouth that knocked Stanley unconscious. Afterwards some of Ketchel's teeth were found embedded in Johnson's glove.

Only one man seemed a possibility to beat Johnson. Big Jim Jeffries, the boilermaker, 6 feet 2 inches and well over 200 pounds, had retired unbeaten as heavyweight champion in 1905 because there was nobody left to beat (he had ignored Johnson). Now he was living well on his alfalfa farm, and in no condition to fight. But the public clamored for Jeffries to come back and lick the upstart, and after several refusals he finally agreed to try. Promoter Tex Rickard put up the unheard-of sum of $101,000 for the fight that gripped all America. It took place at Reno, Nevada, on 4 July 1910.

Jeffries was taller and heavier than Johnson, but at 35 three years older. He was not in the same superb physical condition. Such was his aura, however, that he was made

a 10-6 favorite. This made the action all the more bitter for white Americans to stand. Johnson carved up their idol, laughing his big gold-filled laugh and calling him 'Mistah Jeff.' The referee stopped the fight in the fifteenth with Jeffries down and helpless.

In the next couple of days there were race riots from California in the west to New York in the east. Nineteen people were killed, 250 seriously injured, hundreds more hurt and 5000 arrested. The arrogant Johnson was the most hated man in the country. In the boxing trade there was a desperate search for a 'white hope' to beat him.

It was not boxing that began Johnson's downfall, however. Johnson's second wife committed suicide in despair at his habitual womanizing and Jack immediately married a young white girl. Then it was realized that one white woman had travelled with Jack from state to state as he fulfilled engagements. The Mann Act was a law which forbade transporting a woman across a state line for immoral purposes. Johnson was charged, convicted and sentenced to a year and a day's imprisonment. On bail pending appeal, he crossed to Canada with his new wife and sailed to Europe.

In Paris Jack enjoyed the good life, appearing on the stage and twice defending his title. Then war broke out, and Jack fled to Buenos Aires.

Johnson wanted to return to the States, particularly to see his old mother. A promoter, Jack Curley, suggested to Jack that if he lost the title to Jess Willard, he would be pardoned. There is much controversy about the full details of the deal. In his autobiography Jack claimed that the fight was fixed, that a sum in $500 bills was to be paid at the ringside to his wife after ten rounds, that she would signal to him that she had it and leave, and that he would then lose the fight.

The match took place on the racetrack at Havana, Cuba, on 5 April 1915. Willard was a huge strong cowboy, from Pottawatomie, Kansas, 6 feet 6¼ inches and about 240 pounds. He was not a great fighter, and Jack seemed to control the fight in the early rounds. But no sign came from his wife. The match was scheduled for 45 rounds, and both men looked very tired when, after 25 rounds, Johnson's wife finally gave him the signal and left. In the next round Jack was knocked out.

There have been arguments, allegations and affidavits about this fight ever since, and nobody will ever know for sure if Johnson threw it or was beaten on merit. A famous photograph of him being counted out while apparently shading his eyes from the sun suggests he was quite conscious. On the other hand it would not be surprising if, after 26 rounds in hot sunshine, the 37-year-old had just had enough.

He returned to the States, but was immediately arrested and served the sentence imposed seven years before. His wife divorced him. Without the championship, Jack was now regarded as harmless to white supremacy. He went on boxing till he was 50 years old, and boxed exhibitions when he was 67. He managed a flea circus, ran a gym in New York, and eventually was recognized and universally respected as the great boxer he had been. On 10 June 1946 he died crashing one of the fast cars he loved, and his grave, in Graceland Cemetery, Chicago, is marked simply JOHNSON.

Far left: Jack Johnson in a typical fighting pose.

Right: One of the most discussed photographs in the history of boxing: has Jack Johnson been genuinely knocked out by Jess Willard at Havana in 1915?

Below: Johnson's new wife Etta accompanied him to England in 1911. A year later she committed suicide.

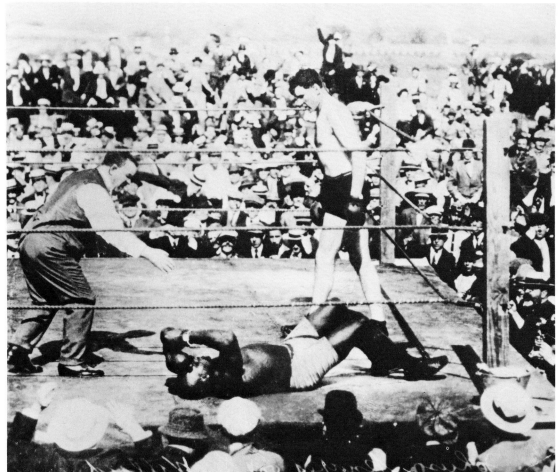

Jack Dempsey
The million-dollar man

For a couple of generations of Americans Jack Dempsey was the epitome of toughness, an all-action, no-quarter-given, out-and-out heavyweight slugger, who at his peak could knock over anybody in the world.

He was born William Harrison Dempsey on 24 June 1895 in Manassa, Colorado. He took the ring name Jack from the old middleweight champion, Jack Dempsey 'The Nonpareil.' He worked in lead mines and lumber camps, did plenty of fighting, turned professional and, although he lost one or two fights while learning his trade, was tough and durable, with a knockout punch in each hand. He went to New York and teamed up with Jack 'Doc' Kearns, a smart young manager and publicist, who, in a stagnant period for heavyweights, secured a match with the champion, Jess Willard.

Dempsey stood 6 feet 1 inch and weighed around 190 pounds, so was at every disadvantage with Willard, more than 5 inches taller and about 50 pounds heavier. But Willard had done little since winning the title except box exhibitions and tour as a cowboy in a circus. The fight was at Toledo on 4 July 1919, and Dempsey and Kearns were so confident that they bet Dempsey's whole purse that he would win in the first round. At first he thought he had. He tore into Willard from the start and knocked him down seven times, finally leaving him helpless on the canvas. Dempsey left the ring in triumph, only to be called back. The time-keeper, using a whistle because the bell was faulty, had blown to end the round and save the champion. Nobody had heard. On the resumption, the unshaven, ferocious Jack continued to batter Jess, who could not come out for the fourth round.

The new champion was not too popular at this time because he had not fought in the war. Promoter Tex Rickard cashed in on this by importing the handsome French war hero Georges Carpentier, the 'Orchid Man.' to meet Dempsey. Skillful publicity – it was called the 'Battle of the Century' – meant that the fight attracted the first million-dollar gate.

Below: **Part of the crowd, the first to pay over $1 million, that saw the Dempsey-Carpentier fight at Jersey City in 1921.**

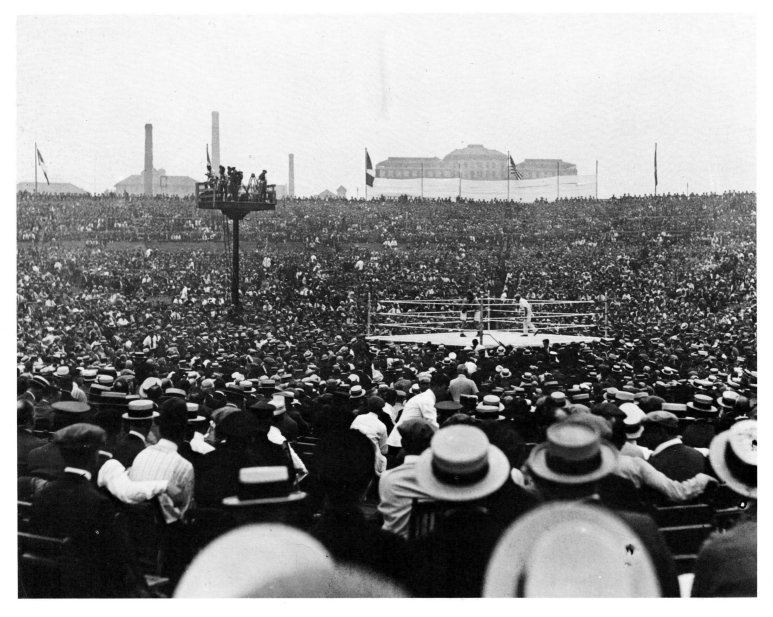

On 2 July 1921, in a specially built open-air arena at Jersey City, 80,183 fans paid $1,789,238 to see the contest with Carpentier, the world light-heavyweight champion. The Orchid Man was no match for the bigger Dempsey and actually broke his thumb on Jack's jaw. Dempsey delivered the knockout in the fourth.

Jack outpointed Tommy Gibbons in a disappointing fight, then drew a second million-dollar gate for a much-hyped match with another giant, the 6 feet 3 inches, 216 pounds Argentinian knockout specialist Luis Firpo, known as the 'Wild Bull of the Pampas.' It was the most

Below: Dempsey during a visit to England.
Bottom: Jack Dempsey with his wife, actress Estelle Taylor, at their new swimming pool before his second Tunney fight.

Above: The champion to be. The young Dempsey posing before his victorious title fight with the giant cowboy Jess Willard.

thrilling heavyweight bout of all, with Firpo down seven times in the first round yet getting up to knock Dempsey clean out of the ring on to the pressmen. They helped Jack back, and he recovered to smash Firpo down for good in the second round.

Having sidestepped Harry Wills, an outstanding black boxer, Dempsey now ran out of challengers, and Kearns arranged for him to make some films in Hollywood. What Kearns did not reckon with was Jack falling for a beautiful young actress, Estelle Taylor. Jack had been disastrously married at 21 and divorced two years later, and now, to Kearns's disgust, he married his movie star. The manager and the wife disliked each other, and when Estelle discovered that Kearns deducted more than half Jack's earnings for expenses, she persuaded her husband to ditch Kearns and put his affairs entirely in the hands of promoter Tex Rickard.

Rickard next matched Dempsey with Gene Tunney at the Sesquicentennial Stadium, Philadelphia, on 23 September 1926. A record paying attendance (to this day) of 120,757 watched the fight in pouring rain. They were in for a big shock. The underrated Tunney skipped round the wet ring and thoroughly outpointed the ring-rusty 31-year-old champion, who remained the fans' favorite. Tunny was booed for his pains. When asked later by his wife what happened Dempsey made the much-quoted remark: 'Honey, I forgot to duck.'

Jack knocked out Jack Sharkey to prove that three years of living more like a pampered movie star than a mauler had not softened him unduly, and was ready for the biggest money-spinner of all – a return with Tunney. On 22 September 1927 104,943 fans packed Soldiers' Field, Chicago, paying a record $2,658,660 for the privilege of being present.

The fight, known as 'The Battle of the Long Count,' is boxing's most famous, because of the controversy in the seventh round. The contest was going the way of the first until then, but suddenly Jack caught up with Tunney on the ropes and four vicious punches put him down. Throughout his career Dempsey had stood over a fallen opponent ready to smash him down again when he got up, and again did just that, despite a ruling that a boxer in such circumstances should retire to a neutral corner. The referee waved Jack away, Jack hesitated, the referee insisted, Jack complied, and only then did the referee take up the count. By the time Tunney scrambled to his feet, he had been down for at least 14 seconds, his head was clear, and he outpointed Jack for the rest of the fight.

Fans argued for years over whether the long count saved Tunney. In any case, Dempsey was cheered from the ring in defeat. When Jack Dempsey died on 31 May 1983 in New York, aged nearly 88, he was as respected as in his heyday in the 1920s.

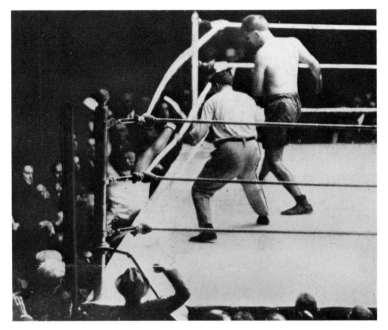

Above: The champion on his way out of the ring against Firpo of Argentina on 14 September 1923.

Left: Dempsey, facing camera, in a fight with Tommy Gibbons on 4 July 1923, which proved financially disastrous for the citizens of Shelby, Montana who backed it.

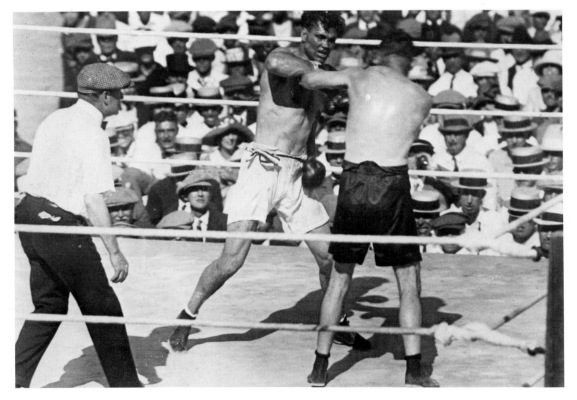

Right: Tunney finds Dempsey with a left in a rain-soaked ring in their first fight at Philadelphia in 1926. A record crowd watched Tunney outpoint the champion.

Gene Tunney
An exemplary career

Gene Tunney brought brains to boxing. He might almost have planned his life in a business career-structure manner from the age of ten, when he asked for a pair of boxing gloves for his birthday. All went very well from there until he died a rich man in his eighties.

James Joseph Tunney was born on 25 May 1897 in Greenwich Village, New York. Unlike most fighters, his was not a poor family. He did not have to fight for a living, but he enjoyed it, studied all its arts, particularly defense, and turned professional. After a few bouts he joined the US Marines, served in France and became a services champion.

Back in civilian life he was undefeated until taking the world light-heavyweight title from Battling Levinsky. In defending this title, he suffered his only reverse, against the great middleweight Harry Greb, a very rough customer called 'The Human Windmill.' Greb gave Tunney such a beating that he was in bed for a week. It was a measure of Tunney's thoroughness that he worked out how to beat Greb, and did so on four subsequent meetings (Greb was to lose only four other fights out of 294).

Gene worked his way through the heavyweight contenders, beating Georges Carpentier and Tommy Gibbons, and was matched with the champion, Dempsey, on 23 September 1926. The two men were almost identical in height, weight and reach, but whereas Dempsey was a non-stop natural attacking puncher, Gene was a pure boxer. He practiced boxing on the retreat for Dempsey, and carried out his strategy

Above: Gene Tunney shortly after his return to the United States after serving in Europe in the US Marines during the First World War.

perfectly, outpointing his man in a rainsoaked ring at Philadelphia. It was not a popular win, Gene's style being regarded as colorless compared with Dempsey's swashbuckling image.

Dempsey had been out of the ring for three years, and he and his supporters were confident that he could get fitter and regain the title. The return match almost a year later, on 22 September 1927, in Chicago, attracted a second attendance of over 100,000. There were record receipts, and Tunney's purse of $990,445 was the highest any boxer received for a fight until television inflated prize money.

Tunney cleverly outfought Dempsey again until the famous seventh round, when Dempsey's blows sent him crashing down to sit clinging to the second rope with his left hand. Because of Dempsey's slowness to move to a neutral corner the count was not taken up immediately and Tunney was actually down for 14 seconds. Tunney recovered to win, flooring Dempsey himself in the eighth, but the arguments started immediately after the fight. Should Tunney have received his long rest, and would the popular Dempsey have won otherwise? Millions of words have been written on this most controversial 'Battle of the Long Count.'

Tunney always maintained he could have beaten the normal count, and Dempsey 40 years later admitted as much himself. Tunney defended only once more, against Tom Heeney of New Zealand. The match lost money for the promoter. Gene's wife, an heiress, then achieved more success than his parents had had when they tried to dissuade him from becoming a professional boxer – she persuaded him to retire undefeated. He became a successful businessman, and resisted attempts to get him to make a comeback. He was interested in literature and enjoyed the friendship of George Bernard Shaw. It was a good life, and in the fashion of heavyweight champions, a long one. He died on 7 November 1978, aged 81.

Above: 'The Battle of the Long Count': Tunney begins to sink to the canvas under Dempsey's onslaught on 22 September 1927 in Chicago.

Left: Dempsey moves in as Tunney begins to rise some 14 seconds or more after the knockdown during 'The Battle of the Long Count.'

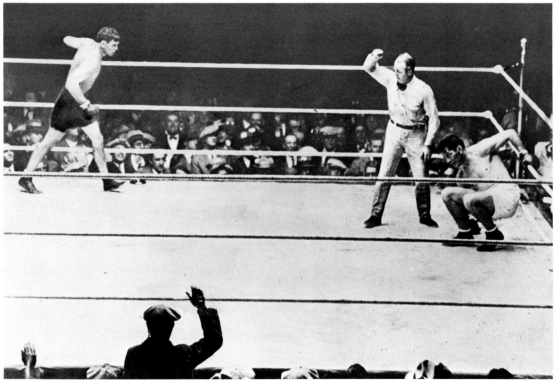

Top far right: Max Schmeling's successful defense of the title in 1931. Young Stribling falls to the champion's power in the last round.

Right: Max Schmeling, the only German world heavyweight champion.

Max Schmeling
Victim of propaganda

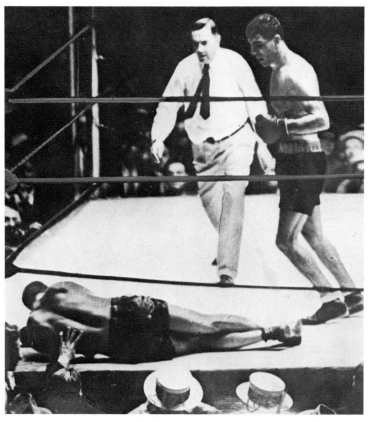

Max Schmeling needed a public relations company working for him. For most people he is the German comprehensively destroyed in one round by Joe Louis in 1938, symbolic of the black man and the free world putting Nazism in its place as the World War brewed. That Schmeling was, in fact, a good boxer who was world champion, and a good sportsman who had previously beaten Louis and much later helped Louis when he met rough times, is much less known.

Max Schmeling was born on 28 September 1905 in

Brandenburg, Germany. He grew big and strong, took up boxing, turned professional in 1924 and was good enough to win the German light-heavyweight title. In June 1927 he won the European title. When Tunney retired, leaving the world heavyweight title vacant, Max and his manager, Arthur Bulow, went to America to campaign. It was a bad decision for Bulow, who was ousted by Joe Jacobs, a mercurial American-Jewish manager. Jacobs took over Schmeling and obtained a match with Jack Sharkey, the 'Boston Gob,' for the vacant championship.

Neither man had the attraction of Dempsey, although the black-haired, beetle-browed Schmeling strangely looked like him. Despite the boxers' lack of charisma, ballyhoo drew 77,116 fans to Yankee Stadium in New York on 12 June 1930. They were disappointed. In the third round Schmeling appeared to be almost out under a Sharkey assault, but in the fourth he found a right uppercut that shook Sharkey and inspired the American to a frenzy. Always a strong body puncher, he suddenly hit Schmeling very low and the German rolled around the canvas helplessly clutching his groin.

In the confusion that followed, Jacobs won the title for his man by leaping into the ring screaming at the officials for a foul, and eventually Schmeling was given the verdict on a disqualification, the only man to win the title in this manner. A year later Max stopped the much lighter Young Stribling in the fifteenth and last round, and then bowed to mounting public pressure to give Sharkey a return.

At Long Island, New York, on 21 June 1932, Sharkey outpointed Schmeling after a dull fight, in which Schmeling could not land his famous right hand to effect. But it was a split decision with much bitter dispute, and many thought Max had won the fight.

Max next proved too strong for former middleweight

23

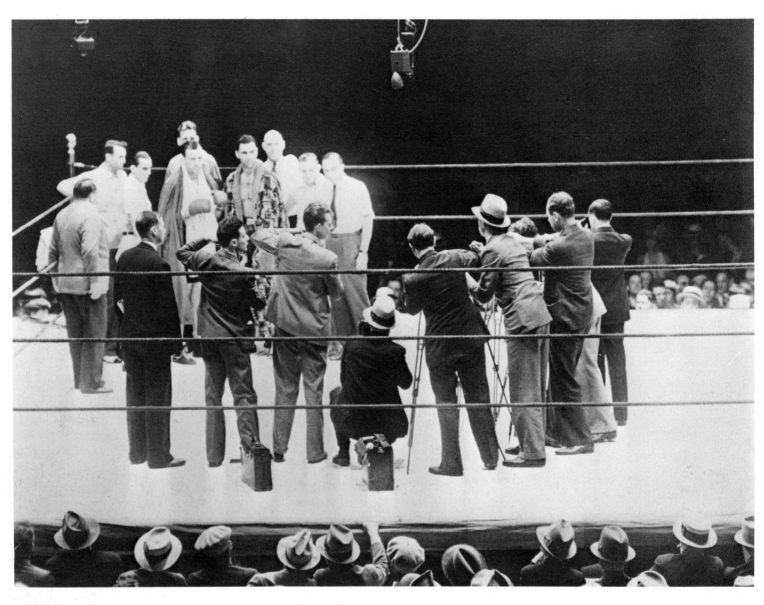

Above: Two years after becoming the only boxer to win the world heavyweight championship on a disqualification, Schmeling lost to Sharkey (left) in New York on 21 June 1932. *Below:* Schmeling covering up against Louis in New York in 1937 in the most famous victory of the German's career.

champion, Mickey Walker, but was stopped by the future heavyweight champion, Max Baer. He won some fights in Europe, and then was invited back to New York to face the unbeaten sensation, Joe Louis. Schmeling, now past 30 years old, was chosen as a safe rung on Louis's ladder to the top, but the experienced ex-champion had spotted a flaw in Louis's technique. In the fourth his right put Louis on the floor for the first time in his career, and in the twelfth, when he gave an encore, Louis could not rise and was counted out.

It was one of the biggest shocks of boxing history, and Schmeling was matched with James J Braddock for another attempt on the world title. But with the prospect of war looming Americans did not want the championship disappearing to Germany. Braddock was persuaded into a deal with Louis which sidestepped Schmeling and Louis became the next champion.

To his credit, Louis was not content until he had beaten Schmeling, and on 22 June 1938 Max was given his chance in New York. He was now nearly 33, Louis was a different proposition, and Max was comprehensively knocked out in 2 minutes 4 seconds.

After serving as a paratrooper in the war, Max made a short comeback and then retired from boxing to look after his business interests.

Joe Louis

Record number of title victories

There is a generation of boxing followers prepared to swear that Joe Louis was the best boxer there ever was. He would certainly figure in nearly everybody's list of contenders. He was almost without a weakness and won more world title fights than any other man.

Joseph Louis Barrow was born in Lafayette, Alabama, on 13 May 1914, of Cherokee Indian stock. His family moved to Detroit, where Joe's mother gave him money for violin lessons in the belief that in hard times a musician could always earn. After a few lessons, Joe preferred to spend the money learning to box in a gymnasium.

He began an amateur career, losing occasionally but winning most, until he turned professional in 1934. A local businessman, John Roxborough, looked after him

Right: Joe Louis completely ruled the heavyweight division from 1937, remaining unbeaten for over ten years.
Below: The knockout with which Louis won the title in 1937. James J Braddock tries to soften his fall in the eighth round.

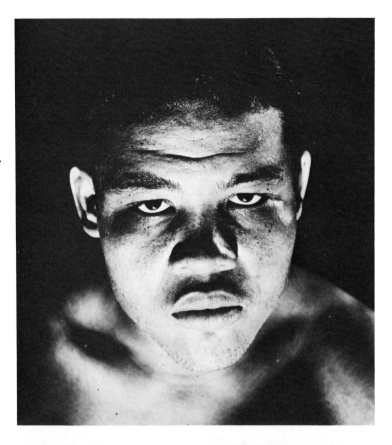

and shortened his name to Joe Louis. Joe rattled up a number of quick wins, which attracted the attention of Mike Jacobs, a ticket speculator, who took over the running of his career and eventually gained control of the promotion of most heavyweight title fights through deals involving his boxer.

Louis, coached by Jack Blackburn, an old black boxer, proved a good pupil, learning a technique of shuffling forward behind a left, and watching for openings for either hand. Each fist carried a knockout punch, earning him the nickname the 'Brown Bomber.' He also had a superb temperament, remaining cool and calculating in the heat of battle. This no doubt helped him learn his last lesson, taught him as he approached contender class. This was to keep a poker face. There was to be no repeat of the Johnson race-hatred. The strategy was successful in that Louis was often described, patronizingly no doubt, as a good ambassador for his race.

Louis proceeded to knock out the best heavyweights, including two recent world champions, Primo Carnera and Max Baer, but when he tackled a third he got the shock of his life. Old-stager Max Schmeling knocked him down and then out.

Above: One of Louis's hardest defenses was his first against Tommy Farr in 1937, two months after winning the title.
Below: The revenge fight with Schmeling: Louis smashes Schmeling to the floor in the first round of their 1938 title fight.

was, and then on 1 March 1949 announced his retirement as unbeaten champion after 25 successful defenses. It was a marvelous record.

Alas, unpaid income tax forced him to return to the ring to earn more, a decision which incidentally lost him his wife, who, hardly ever seeing him during his career, now divorced him for a second time. It also tarnished his great record. Challenging Ezzard Charles, who had assumed the championship, on 27 September 1950, the 36-year-old Louis was outpointed. He then won eight more fights before, on 26 October 1951, becoming cannon fodder for the young Rocky Marciano. The fight took place in New York and Marciano inflicted his second knockout defeat by disposing of Louis in the eighth.

Louis retired again, but sadly was forced to exploit his name by wrestling, and then the man who had earned over $4½ million in the ring became a host at a Las Vegas casino. He died on 12 April 1981.

Louis kept his poker face, and, among others, knocked out another ex-champion, Jack Sharkey. Then Mike Jacobs pulled a master-stroke. He persuaded the reigning world champion, James J Braddock, to ignore an arrangement to fight Schmeling and to accept a challenge from Louis instead. The deal offered was that should Braddock lose he would receive ten percent of the profits of the next ten years' title fights.

Braddock, the 'Cinderella Man,' had surprised even himself by winning the title. After all, he had practically retired in despair once, having lost about a quarter of his 80 fights. Nobody thought Braddock could hold the title for long, and certainly not beat Louis, so it was not surprising that his manager accepted Jacobs's deal. If Braddock received his due, the deal was the best any boxer ever made.

Louis fought Braddock in Chicago on 22 June 1937, and the Cinderella Man surprised the world by dumping Joe on his trunks in the first round. However, Joe got up, fought back and knocked Braddock out in the eighth. He thus became the second black man to win the world heavyweight championship.

Joe Louis then embarked on an amazing run, beating off 21 challenges between August 1937 and March 1942. Some were of little account, and the press dubbed this the 'Bum-of-the-Month' campaign.

But some challengers were top-class. In 1937 Louis had a narrow points win over British champion Tommy Farr, which thrilled millions of the loser's countrymen, listening to the radio commentary from New York in the small hours of the morning – some critics thought that Farr had won this fight. In 1938, there was a devastating one-round revenge victory over Max Schmeling, who, when he caught his ship back to Germany a few days later, was carried aboard on a stretcher. In 1941 former light-heavy king Billy Conn was outboxing Louis and winning until he got cocky and traded punches with the 25 pound heavier champion who knocked him out in the thirteenth.

Louis, who gave purses to navy and army relief, then served as a sergeant instructor in the war, resuming his career in 1946. He won four defenses of his title, two against Jersey Joe Walcott, who was even older than he

Above left: Joe Louis in his last contest as champion, gets his right into Jersey Joe Walcott's face.

Left: Louis in his prime with his championship belt.

Jersey Joe Walcott

Everything comes to he who waits

Jersey Joe Walcott fortified the over-forties better than any proprietary tonic. He won the world heavyweight championship at a time when ordinary men begin to check their pension arrangements.

Arnold Raymond Cream was born in Merchantville, New Jersey, on 31 January 1914. When he began boxing he thought his name did not sound quite right, so he adopted the name of an old ring idol, Joe Walcott, the 'Barbados Demon,' one-time welterweight king, and added Jersey to the front to denote his state. In their prime the two boxers looked remarkably alike.

Joe, who some thought was older than the official record states, was boxing professionally at 16 as a featherweight. He was a good defensive boxer, who moved up the weight divisions as he got older but was not

championship class in any, nor a crowd-pleaser, so in 1944 he retired to look after his wife and six children.

He was working in a soup factory in Camden, New Jersey, when a local operator took a lease on the town's arena and persuaded Joe with $500 and a promise of six fights to put on his fighting togs again and help the arena off to a good start. Walcott won impressively, and went on doing so. He even beat Joe Baksi, a championship contender. The local fans began to crowd in to see him.

In 1947 Jersey Joe was reckoned a good harmless opponent for Joe Louis to box in a 10-round exhibition for charity at Madison Square Garden, scheduled for 5 December. Nobody was killed in the rush to buy tickets, so to increase public interest the fight was extended to 15 rounds with Louis's title at stake. This was the first world heavyweight title fight to be televised. Jersey Joe astonished Louis and the viewers by boxing brilliantly. Louis got the split decision, but even he thought he had lost, and apologised to Jersey Joe for the verdict.

A return was called for, but on 25 June 1948 a sharper Louis knocked out Jersey Joe in the twelfth round. That appeared to be the end of the trail again.

However, Louis retired, and Walcott and Ezzard Charles, the 'Cincinnati Flash,' were chosen to fight for the vacant title. On 22 June 1949, in Chicago, the 35-year-old veteran, who had not fought for a year, was outpointed by the seven-years-younger Charles, so Jersey Joe had been the loser in three consecutive heavyweight title fights, a unique record. But it was a close fight, and after Charles had seen off six challengers, including Louis, in his comeback, Jersey Joe was given another chance. At Detroit on 7 March 1951, Walcott put Charles down, but the final result was the same – a points defeat.

Jersey Joe had made more money in his four losing title shots than in all his previous years of boxing, so when Charles ran out of worthwhile opponents and Joe was invited to try again, he accepted with pleasure. The fight was at Pittsburgh on 18 July 1951, and this time everything was different. He fought with unusual abandon, and in the seventh landed his best punch, a left hook, smack on Ezzard's chin and the lights went out for the champion.

After 21 years in the business, Jersey Joe Walcott was heavyweight champion. At 37½ years old he remains the oldest to have won the title. On 5 June 1952 he gave Charles a return in Philadelphia and outpointed him. He was now earning big money. His next defense was on 23 September, also in Philadelphia. Nobody gave him a chance against the rough, unbeaten Rocky Marciano but within a minute the old campaigner's left hook put Rocky on the floor for the first time in his life. Joe continued to outpoint Rocky, and was winning with ease, but the

Above: 37-year-old Jersey Joe Walcott wipes away a tear as he is presented with his world championship belt by the publisher of *Ring* magazine, Nat Fleischer, in 1951.

Left: Walcott emphasizes his claim to the crown with a successful defense against the previous heavyweight champion, Ezzard Charles, at Philadelphia in 1952.

Right: Jersey Joe Walcott, the happy family man, with his wife Lydia and their six children, after he had come out of retirement and taken Louis the distance. The title was yet to come.

amazingly strong challenger, nearly ten years his junior, kept coming forward and in the thirteenth caught up with him. A terrific swing left Jersey Joe sliding down the ropes to be counted out with his face on the canvas.

He took the contractual return, but on 15 May 1953 in Chicago was dispatched in the first round, perhaps the best thing that could have happened in the circumstances. His next birthday would be his 40th, not an age to be mixing it for long with perhaps the most brutal puncher ever seen in a ring.

Joe went back to his wife and six children with no need now to look for laboring jobs. He refereed the second Ali-Liston title fight, but made a mess of its controversial ending. More happily he was mayor of Camden. A religious man, who would pray before fights, he was also attached to the New Jersey Police, helping to fight juvenile delinquency.

Left: Superfit Jersey Joe Walcott in training.
Below (sequence): Jersey Joe is ready to rise after a punch from the new champion Rocky Marciano in the first round of the fight held in Chicago in 1953. Walcott lost the fight, his manager later claiming Jersey Joe had been counted out at nine.

Rocky Marciano
The perfect record

Rocky Marciano was the most primitive champion of modern times. He had only one method – to get into the ring and batter his opponent into insensibility as quickly as possible. And he did not care too much where his blows landed. He was amazingly successful. Eighty-eight percent of his opponents were knocked out, among the highest percentage of all champions.

Rocky was born of poor Italian parents in Brockton, Massachusetts, on 1 September 1923. He was Rocco Francis Marchegiano, and his first big fight was with pneumonia. He almost died when 19 months old from what was then frequently a fatal illness.

In March 1943 Rocky was drafted into the army. For a while he was stationed in Britain, and legend has it that it was flattening an Australian in a Cardiff pub that sparked his interest in boxing. He began in the army,

Above: Marciano's power proves too much for the ageing ex-champ, Joe Louis, in a fight held in New York in 1951.
Below: Ezzard Charles (left) was the only challenger to take Marciano the distance in a title fight. The ferocity of the exchanges can be seen from the marks on the fighters' faces as they battle in New York in June 1954.

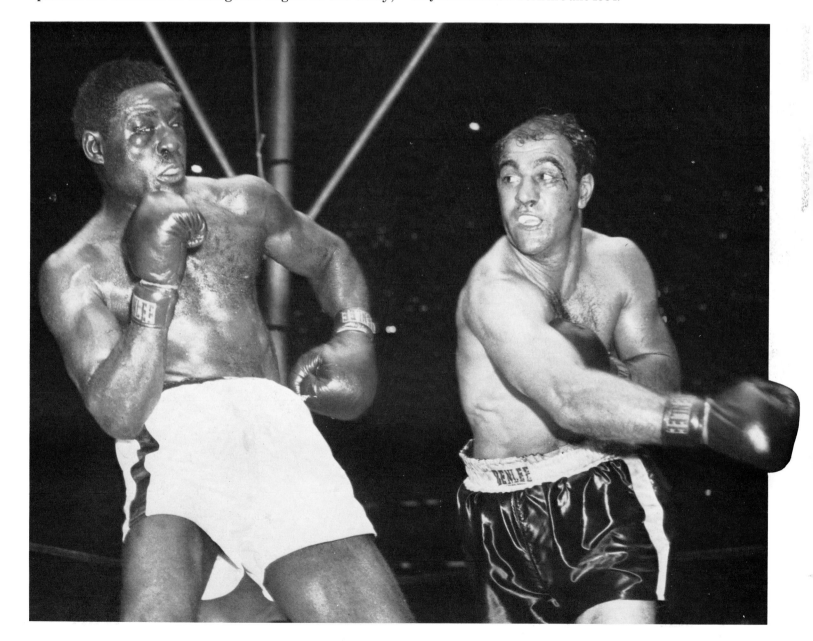

where he also played baseball (his first love), and when on leave in 1946 had his first public fight as an amateur, ignominiously being disqualified after kneeing his opponent in the groin in the second round because he was too tired to hold up his arms.

He got into better condition to begin a professional career in March 1947. He did not need much stamina, as it was not until his thirteenth fight two years later that he was taken beyond the third round. He wrote to Al Weill, a well-known manager, for a trial, was invited to New York, and Weill, somewhat reluctantly, took him on. At not quite 5 feet 11 inches, weighing 184 pounds (only a cruiserweight by today's categories), with short arms and no science, he did not look much of a prospect.

Rocky had seen off 22 opponents in only 62 rounds before Weill got him a fight in New York. Rocky won in the second. His opponents got better in class, until on 26 October 1951 he fought the legendary Joe Louis, who was attempting a comeback. Rocky knocked him out in the eighth and ended the old warrior's career. Quick knockouts of Lee Savold and Harry 'Kid' Matthews followed, and on 23 September 1952 at Philadelphia Rocky challenged the venerable Jersey Joe Walcott for the championship of the world. He had had only 42 fights, all wins, but because of his late start was already in his 30th year.

The contest was a fair summary of Rocky's style. He soaked up punishment (Walcott put him down for the first time), but just kept coming forward, relentlessly clubbing in blows of all types and from all angles, until enough got through to sink his opponent. With Walcott it came in the thirteenth, Rocky's longest fight to date.

Rocky knocked out Walcott in the first round in a return. Most boxers who took on Rocky twice subsided more quickly the second time, as if the first experience had weakened their resolve. Roland LaStarza was knocked out in the eleventh round in New York in 1953 after a gallant display – he had taken Rocky the distance three years before.

In 1954 Rocky twice fought former champion Ezzard Charles. The first contest was Rocky's hardest. He took a 15-round decision, but Charles fought all the way, Rocky getting on top only in the last five rounds, and even he was exhausted at the end. In the fourth Charles had opened a gash by Rocky's left eye which spurted blood, and which almost caused the fight to be stopped.

In the return Charles soaked up punishment until the knockout blow arrived in the eighth round, but again the fight might have been stopped in his favor. Two rounds earlier he had split Marciano's left nostril, and there was no way the blood could be prevented from spurting like a geyser all over Rocky, his opponent and the ring. The doctor let the champion continue, but would have been forced to stop it had Rocky not won in that hectic eighth round.

Marciano lost a little ambition after this. The British champion, Don Cockell, took him on in San Francisco in 1955. Cockell was shorter and stubbier even than Marciano, and put up a good show before succumbing in the ninth round. But in this fight Marciano was wilder than ever before, delivering several blows which would have earned disqualification in a British ring.

Archie Moore, the experienced light-heavyweight champion, was the last challenger, on 21 September 1955 in New York. Archie was already nearly 39, if you believed him – his mother maintained he was three years older than the published record. Clever old Archie dumped Rocky on his hands and knees in the second, but was worn down and knocked out in the ninth round.

Seven months later Marciano decided to retire, and stuck to his decision, refusing huge financial offers to make a comeback. He had earned around $4 million, and seemed to have been careful with it – although he was not a businessman, and when his affairs came to be sorted out the disappearance of much of the money was a mystery. His record was perfect: 49 wins in 49 fights, 43 inside the distance. He is the only heavyweight champion never to have been beaten in his career.

Rocky's belligerence in the ring has never been equalled, but outside the ring he was a gentle and modest family man. He wore a toupee under a hat, which once blew off at a public function, carrying the hairpiece with it. This tremendously tough slugger blushed crimson and ran away.

On the eve of his 46th birthday Rocky was flying to a business meeting. The aircraft in which he was travelling crashed at Newton, Iowa, and he was killed.

Right: **British challenger Don Cockell (right) near the end of his gallant resistance to Marciano's relentless and often reckless punching in San Francisco in 1955.**
Below: **A hint of the power in Rocky Marciano's fists and forearms is given by this pose from his title days.**

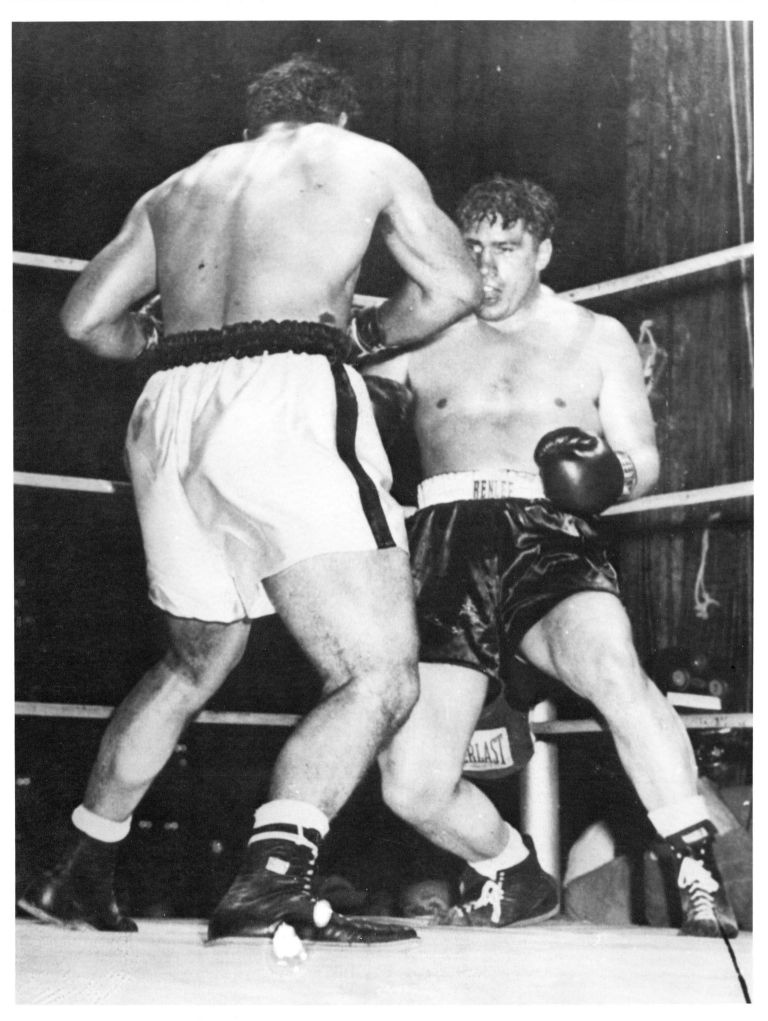

Floyd Patterson
Master of disguise

Floyd Patterson was a contradictory character. He established two very distinguished records in heavyweight boxing. He was the youngest-ever champion and the first man in history to regain the title. Yet for the top man in the world he was at times strangely tentative and lacking in confidence. The brooding, menacing Liston seemed to frighten him out of the championship.

Floyd Patterson was born on 4 January 1935 at Waco, North Carolina, the third son of a laborer who soon took the family to Brooklyn. In this tough area of New York Floyd played truant, was a retarded pupil and was sent to a reform school, where he learned to box. When he joined his older brothers' amateur club at 14, he cried on being hurt. Nevertheless he tagged along to the gym when his

brothers turned professional, and so improved his boxing that he won a Golden Gloves championship and then, at 17, the 1952 Olympic middleweight gold medal, knocking out his Romanian opponent in the final in 74 seconds.

Patterson turned professional three months later, and, still growing, made rapid progress into the heavyweight contender class. When Marciano retired Patterson had lost only once, to the former light-heavyweight champion, Joey Maxim. He won an eliminator, and then climbed in with veteran Archie Moore for the vacant title. On 30 November 1956, in Chicago, Floyd knocked out Archie in the fifth.

At 21 years, 10 months and 26 days, he became the youngest to win the title, a record he held until Mike Tyson knocked out Trevor Berbick in 1986. At only just 6 feet and barely 190 pounds, Floyd was hardly a true heavyweight. Only Marciano of the champions has had a shorter reach. Floyd cultivated a personal style. He hid behind his arms, peering round them in what was called his 'peek-a-boo' style. He would attack by launching himself from the floor like a rocket, rattling rapid

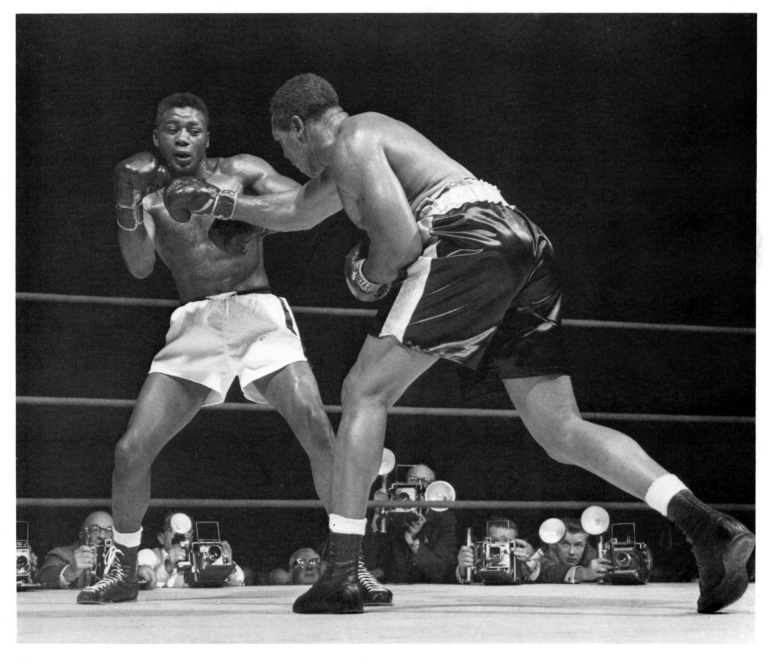

punches to his opponent's chin. Nobody put punches together faster than Floyd.

Cus d'Amato, his manager, picked easy opponents for him for his first four defenses, and probably thought Ingemar Johansson, of Sweden, would be a fifth. Patterson was a 4-1 favorite to beat him at Yankee Stadium, New York, on 26 June 1959, but the Swede had a terrific right which kept landing on Floyd's jaw in the third round. The champion was up and down like a rubber ball six times before the referee decided that the seventh knockdown was sufficient. This was a very significant fight in that for the first time the television receipts were very much higher than the gate. A new era in the history of boxing had begun, leading to the eventual domination of the sport by television interests.

Patterson then showed his retiring nature by going into hiding for a year before taking the contractual return at the Polo Grounds, New York, on 20 June 1960. This time Floyd leapt in and punished the statuesque Swede on the body before, in the fifth, switching to the head and knocking him out. He thus claimed his second

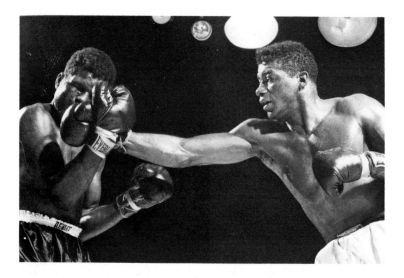

Above: Tommy Jackson takes a right from Patterson.
Left: Patterson (facing camera) became the youngest champion in 1956. Archie Moore was knocked out in the fifth.
Below: A fifth-round knockout was also the means by which Patterson regained the title from Johansson in June 1960.

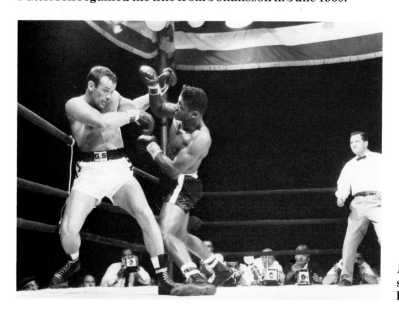

Right: Floyd Patterson, whose style was fast, skillful and highly individual.

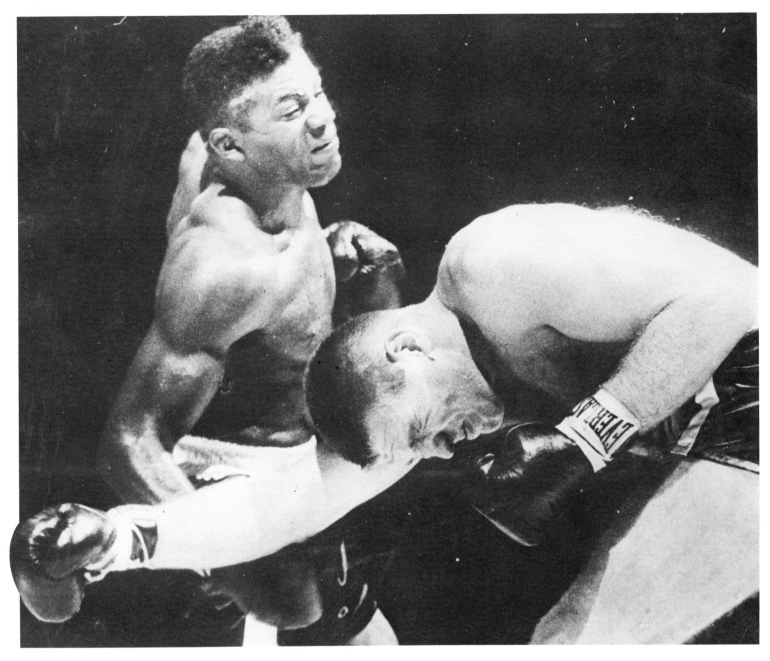

Above: Patterson screws up his face in effort, while Tom McNeeley screws his up in pain, after a right to the body from Patterson in his last successful defense in Toronto in 1961.

record. He was the first man, although many had tried, to win back the championship.

Naturally there had to be a decider between the two men and this took place at the Convention Hall, Miami Beach, on 13 March 1961. This was a very exciting fight, with both getting their best punches in. Patterson was twice down in the first round, but this time got up and put Johansson down. Few thought he could recover like this, and his recovery was complete when finally he knocked the challenger out in the sixth.

Floyd next disposed of Tom McNeeley, but in the background all this while was Sonny Liston, a bigger, heavier man who exuded malice and was built up by the press as unbeatable. Patterson seemed to believe this because when he was finally forced to meet Liston at Comiskey Park, Chicago, on 25 September 1962, Floyd seemed mesmerized. He hardly had time to make any moves

before Liston's huge fists had smashed him to the canvas. The match lasted 2 minutes 6 seconds.

It was said in boxing circles that part of Patterson's fighting gear was a false beard and spectacles, so that if he lost he could slip out of a back door unrecognized. He never needed his Lon Chaney kit more than on this night, unless it was in the return. This took place ten months later, at the Convention Hall, Las Vegas, on 22 July 1963. Poor Floyd lasted only four more seconds than he had in the first fight.

This might have seemed the end of his career, but the brave Patterson fought on and actually challenged for the title twice more. On 22 November 1965 he took on Muhammad Ali, but, boxing with an injured back, he took a terrible beating before the referee saved him in the twelfth. On 14 September 1968, when 33, he lost on points to Jimmy Ellis, the WBA champion, in Stockholm. Two years later he made a comeback and won nine fights but he then met Ali again, himself on the comeback trail, and lost in seven rounds. After 21 years as a professional Floyd finally decided this was enough.

Ingemar Johansson
Business with pleasure

When Ingemar Johansson arrived at New York from Sweden for his first world heavyweight title fight with Floyd Patterson, the American boxing scribes met the boat and were introduced to his party: his father, the trainer; his mother, the cook; brother Rolf, sparring partner; Rolf's girl friend, Annette; his sister Eva and brother Henry, consultants; and Birgit Lundgren, secretary and fiancée. The fistic scribblers looked at each other and shook their heads. When the whole party moved into training camp together, and Ingemar's idea of training seemed to include a dally by the swimming pool with Birgit, followed by an evening meal and a dance, they shook their heads even more. This was not the monk-like seclusion and masculine meanness of the usual big fight preparation. Mr Johansson was something else.

Ingemar Johansson, born 16 October 1932 in Gothenburg, was used to upsetting the experts, even at the Olympic Games. In 1952, when Patterson won the middleweight gold medal, Ingemar had reached the heavyweight final. But he seemed so apprehensive of the punching power of Ed Sanders (USA) that he just did not fight, and in the second round was sensationally disqualified for not trying. He even forfeited the silver medal (he was finally given it 30 years later). Strangely the fearsome Sanders was to die two years later of a brain hemorrhage after being knocked out in his ninth professional fight – it was Johansson who went on to greater things.

After his disgrace, Ingemar turned professional and won the European heavyweight title by knocking out

Above: Ingemar Johansson, of Sweden, the last white undisputed heavyweight champion of the world.

Right: Johansson winning the title, and putting Floyd Patterson on the canvas for one of his seven knockdowns at New York on 26 June 1959.

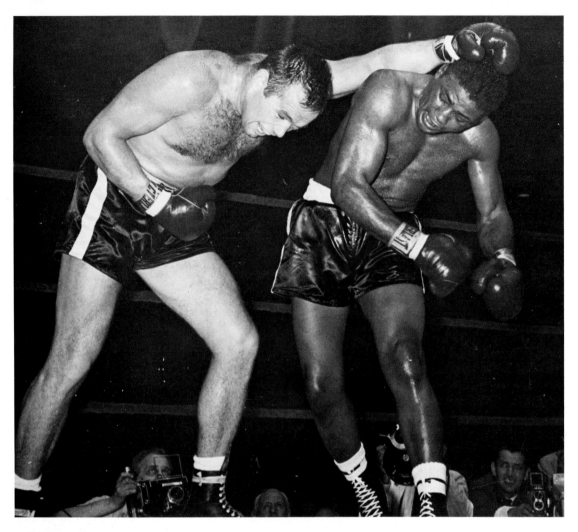

Far right, above: The new champion Sonny Liston, the 'Ugly Bear,' at a lunch in his honor in London in 1963.

Far right, below: Patterson has been knocked out by Sonny Liston in the first round at Chicago on 25 September 1962: Liston consoles him while Liston's seconds move in to celebrate with the new champion.

Left: Johansson's second title fight was against Floyd Patterson in Miami in 1961. Patterson disposed of Johansson in the sixth in what proved a dramatic and exciting fight.

Below left: World champion Ingemar with his fiancée, Birgit Lundgren, who was never far from his side even when he was preparing for his big fights.

Italian Franco Cavicchi, a treatment he also handed out to Henry Cooper. When he knocked out top-ranking American Eddie Machen in 2 minutes 16 seconds, the imposing 6 foot, 200 pound Swede won his title shot with Patterson.

The scribes who met Ingemar's boat and chronicled his training naturally gave him no chance, but not for the first time the experts were wrong. On 26 June 1959 at the Yankee Stadium, New York, Ingemar surprised them all, plus the punters who made Patterson 4-1 favorite, and especially Patterson himself, when he displayed an explosive right hand and crashed a bemused Patterson to the canvas seven times in the third to take the title.

The scribes who had been so dismissive now rushed to nickname the right hand punch of the new champion. 'The Hammer of Thor' was the choice of those with a classical bent; those of a more popular readership settled for 'Ingo's Bingo.'

Naturally there was great interest in the return held at the New York Polo Grounds a year later. Ingo was a firm favorite this time at 8-5 but a more determined Patterson knocked out an over-confident Swede. Floyd also won the rubber match, and Ingemar's world aspirations were at an end.

Johansson regained the European crown, but retired at 31 to do what he probably enjoyed most. He became a businessman, adding to the $1½ million he had made from his title fights, and went to live in the tax haven of Switzerland with the glamorous Birgit.

Sonny Liston
The Ugly Bear

Sonny Liston had a face which might have guaranteed stardom in horror movies: a stony expression, with cold, brooding, threatening eyes. Liston used it in the war of nerves at the weigh-in and the pre-fight instructions of the referee, glowering at his opponent. His whole demeanor was of menace. No doubt the fear he inspired helped him win some of his fights.

Charles Liston was born in a shanty town at St Francis, Arkansas, on 8 May 1932. His father, a farmhand, allegedly sired 25 children. Liston ran away to St Louis at 13 years old, and was in trouble with the law more or less throughout his teens. Armed robbery landed him in a Missouri penitentiary where a chaplain directed Liston's energies into boxing. He won a Golden Gloves tournament in 1953 and turned professional, but unfortunately came under the influence of the gangster element on the fringe of boxing.

Liston had all the physical attributes of a future heavyweight champion. He was 6 feet 1 inch and 216

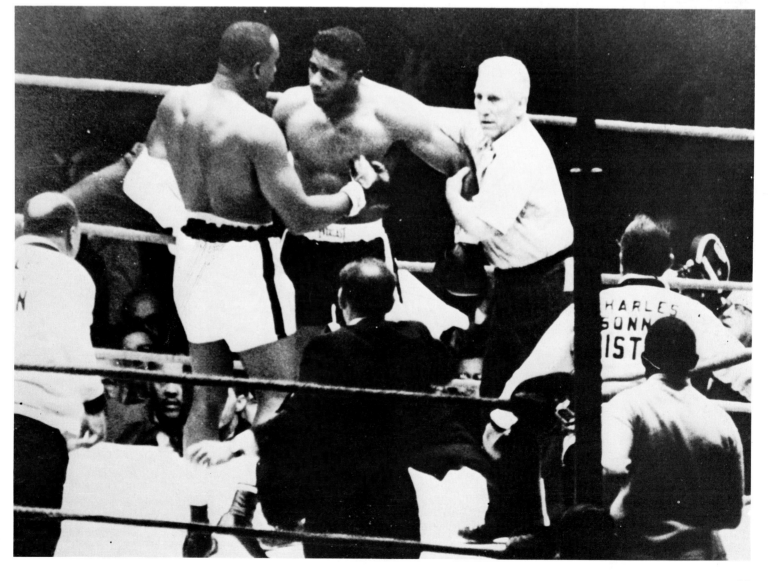

pounds and had a long reach and enormous fists. He lost his seventh contest to Marty Marshall, who broke Liston's jaw halfway through the fight – Liston nevertheless lost only on points. This was the only blot on his early boxing record, and he avenged it twice, but his career received a setback when he assaulted a policeman and was imprisoned for nine months.

On his return to the ring he eliminated all the contenders and, although many boxing officials did not want a man with his record fighting for the title, he eventually proved himself the outstanding challenger.

He fought champion Floyd Patterson on 25 September 1962 at Chicago. New York had refused the bout because of Liston's unsavory reputation. Sonny had a physical advantage of 25 pounds in weight and 13 inches in reach, and possibly an immeasurable psychological advantage too. He ignored Patterson's apprehensive lefts and just bulldozed in with a series of savage body blows which ended only when he slung a vicious left hook to Patterson's chin. Patterson was lifted off his feet and crashed to the canvas from where he had no chance of getting up. It was all over in one round. At the Convention Hall in Las Vegas ten months later, Sonny repeated the one-round treatment, and looked invincible.

But Sonny had taken a long time to win his crown, and was now 31 years old. His next challenger was a brash, superfit phenomenon of 22, Cassius Clay. Clay himself was a master of psychological warfare, and dubbed

Liston the 'Ugly Bear.' Clay had had only 20 fights, however, and was 7-1 against when the two met at Miami Beach on 25 February 1964. Clay, a superb physical specimen at 6 feet 3 inches and 215 pounds, was one opponent who was not inferior to Liston in stature. But mentally? At the weigh-in Clay's pulse was racing and his blood pressure was 200/100. The fight was almost called off. The consensus was that Clay was scared out of his life.

Clay fought well enough, however, and Liston failed to nail him. After six rounds Clay was getting in punches at long range. Suddenly Liston looked old and fallible. When the bell rang for the start of the seventh round he remained sullenly on his stool, claiming a shoulder injury and conceding his title.

If the scribes were unhappy at this sudden ending, they were openly cynical about the return. On 25 May 1965 at Lewiston, Maine, Sonny was knocked out after one minute with a punch that most did not see and many believed did not take place. Was this Liston snubbing authority once again? He had taken part in four world title fights, winning two, losing two, and three had ended in the first round.

After a year Sonny made a comeback and carried on until 1970. But on 30 December 1970 he died mysteriously. His wife discovered his body six days later in his Las Vegas kitchen. Even in death the taciturn Liston had been a loner.

Left: The power of Liston: a right uppercut coming from somewhere near knee-level will soon make contact with the body of the champion, Patterson. Liston's victory at Chicago on 25 September 1962 came in just over two minutes of the first round.

Right: One of the most ignoble ends to a world title fight: Sonny Liston lies on his back after taking a blow from Muhammad Ali, who stands snarling above him. The fight, held at Lewiston, Maine in 1965, brought another first round finish to a Liston fight.

Henry Cooper
A famous left hook

Muhammad Ali was never knocked out, and in his prime, before he lost three years of his career over his draft refusal, there was never any danger that he would be. Except once. Henry Cooper's left hook had him down and glassy-eyed, his senses gone. Only three things saved Ali from being knocked out: the bell, illegal smelling salts, and a split which mysteriously appeared in his glove, causing a long enough delay between rounds for him to recover his senses. It was nevertheless Cooper's finest moment in a glittering career.

Henry Cooper was the older of identical twins born in a Westminster hospital on 3 May 1934. Both became amateur and then professional boxers, based at Bellingham, on the outskirts of London. Henry was the better fighter, turning professional in 1954, and doing well enough to take part in a British heavyweight title eliminator, in which he was outpointed by Joe Erskine. At 6 feet and 190 pounds Cooper was a fast, slim heavyweight with a hard left hook. But he also had prominent bones and thin skin tissue around the eyes and lost many fights through cuts.

From 1956 to 1958 he had a disastrous run, losing five and drawing one of seven contests. The tide turned in a fight with Dick Richardson, later European champion. The rough Richardson cut Cooper's eye in the first and put him down in the fifth, but Henry got up and knocked Richardson clean off his feet with his left hook, and that was that. In his next fight Zora Folley, a highly ranked

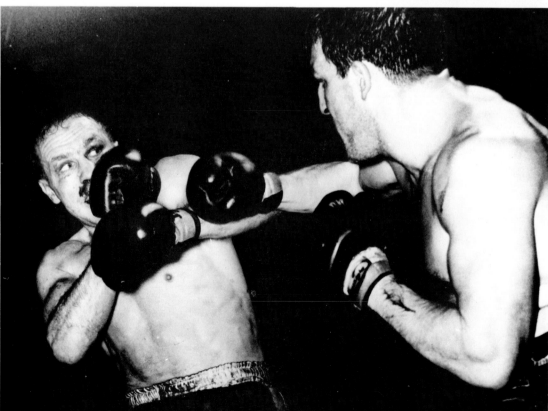

Above: Henry Cooper at the beginning of a long and successful professional career which saw him as British champion for over ten years and the only boxer to win outright three Lonsdale belts.

Left: Cooper (left) covering up against British champion Brian London at Earls Court in January 1959. Henry won on points to win the title.

Right: Cooper's handicap is only too obvious in his world title fight with Muhammad Ali in 1966. Cooper gave Ali plenty of trouble in their two fights, and it was Cooper's tendency to cut around the eyes which was decisive on both occasions. The referee was forced to intervene in this fight to save Cooper from possible permanent injury.

American, was outpointed, and in the next, on 12 January 1959, he took the British and Empire heavyweight titles from Brian London.

He was still champion when, in 1963, he met Ali, then known as Cassius Clay. Clay had cut Cooper's eye in the third, and it was in the fourth that the bell rescued Clay. After the business with the split glove, Clay went to work on Cooper's eye again and the fight was stopped in the fifth. According to Cooper, Clay was still using the glove with the stuffing hanging out which was, of course, very damaging to a bad cut.

Cooper met Ali again on 21 May 1966 when Ali was world champion. Cooper was always confident of handling Ali, and was doing well until the sixth, when a chopping blow split an eye and blood gushed profusely. The referee had no option but to stop the fight.

Henry remained British and Empire champion until 1969 by which time he was also European champion. He was even Boxer of the Year in Italy. He had been British and Empire champion for a record ten years and picked up three Lonsdale belts, the only man to do so.

Cooper was then matched with Jimmy Ellis for the WBA world title. But the British Boxing Board of Control, who supported the rival WBC, refused to recognize the contest as for the championship. Cooper resigned his British and Empire titles on 28 May 1969 in protest, and on 9 October gave up the European title, too, a cartilage operation preventing him defending it.

He made a comeback in 1970, immediately winning back the British and Commonwealth titles from Jack Bodell, and the European title from Jose Urtain of Spain.

On 16 March 1971 Cooper, rising 37, put all three titles on the line against Joe Bugner, and lost on points in one of the most criticized and resented decisions any referee ever made. He gave up swapping punches then and went into the celebrity business, remaining ever since one of the best-known and liked personalities in Britain.

Above: One young strong boxer who threatened Cooper's supremacy during his long reign was blond, hard-punching Billy Walker. Cooper, however, proved too skillful, and the referee stopped their 1967 fight at Wembley in Cooper's favor in the sixth round. This win brought Cooper his third Lonsdale belt.

Right: After giving up the title following a dispute with the British Boxing Board of Control, Cooper regained it at the first opportunity in 1970 when he outpointed the man who had assumed his crown, Jack Bodell.

44

Muhammad Ali
Simply 'The Greatest'

Muhammad Ali kept boxing fans throughout the world thoroughly entertained for 20 years. Not only did he have a superb physique and outstanding courage and boxing skills, he was better at publicity than Madison Avenue, he was a wit, poet, prophet, university lecturer and for a while the best-known fighter in the world. He called himself 'The Greatest' and not many thought of arguing with him.

He was born Cassius Marcellus Clay in Louisville, Kentucky, on 17 January 1942. When he was 12 he tearfully reported a stolen bicycle to the police, and the patrolman enrolled him in his gym to learn boxing. He was good, won Golden Gloves championships, and then the 1960 Olympic light-heavyweight title in Rome. He was so proud of his gold medal that he would not be parted from it, wearing it always. But when, back in Louisville, he was refused a hamburger at a whites-only restaurant, his patriotism evaporated and he threw the medal into the Ohio river.

Eleven white men, mostly millionaires, sponsored him as a professional, with Angelo Dundee as his trainer. The brilliant Cassius built up a big reputation and added spice to his progress by predicting, often in verse, the round in which his opponent would fall. He was remarkably accurate, too.

All this from such a young man did not endear him to everyone, especially when he knocked out the respected 'Ancient Archie' Moore, who had been boxing professionally seven years before Clay was born. In fact he was universally disliked as a braggart, and given various nicknames. Eventually the 'Louisville Lip' won the popularity stakes over 'Gaseous Cassius' and 'Mighty Mouth.' People waited impatiently for the lip of the controversial and outspoken boxer to be buttoned.

Clay predicted he would be world champion before he

Below left: Cassius Clay, as he was then known, getting the upper hand against Sonny Liston in the sixth round of their world championship match in 1964.
Below right: Cassius Clay, aged 12, world champion-to-be.

Left: The young Cassius Clay. When he won a gold medal at the 1960 Olympic Games in Rome, he was a light-heavyweight. Later Clay threw the medal away in protest against racism in the United States.

Below: After disposing of Liston, Ali gave the ubiquitous Floyd Patterson a bad beating over 12 rounds at Las Vegas in 1965.

Right above: In 1974 Ali fought Ernie Terrell, whom the WBA had named champion when Ali had changed his name and assumed his new religious stance. Ali gave Terrell a humiliating drubbing to unify the championship again.

Right below: A poster for the championship fight in Kinshasa, Zaire.

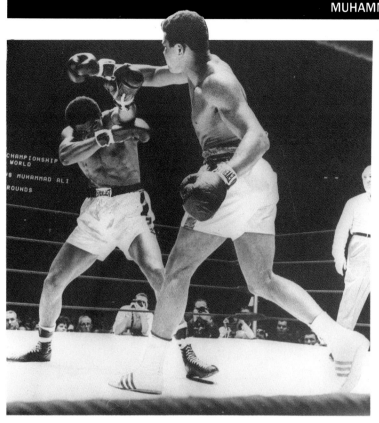

operation for acute hernia, after his stomach had swelled like a football. 'It could have been worse,' growled Liston. 'It could have been me.'

The fight was a farce, Liston being knocked out in round one without apparently being hit hard enough to knock out Miss World. There were cries of 'Fix' and 'Fake,' and the astonishing episode has never been satisfactorily explained.

Ali proved an excellent champion, taking on the best and defending impressively nine times in less than two years. Two bouts left a bad taste. One was a terrible beating of former champion Floyd Patterson, whom Ali taunted with cries of 'Uncle Tom' as he speared his punches in. The second was with Ernie Terrell, whom the WBA had installed as their champion, having withdrawn recognition of Ali when he changed his name. Terrell insisted on calling his opponent Clay, and Ali punished him mercilessly throughout the whole 15 rounds, interspersing punches with the question 'What's my name?'

Ali, meanwhile, had been in dispute with the US Army draft board, claiming deferment from service as a Muslim minister, but on 9 May 1967 he was indicted for failing to submit to the draft. The boxing authorities

was 21, but in fact had to wait until he was just past 22 before he got his chance – and that was against the fearsome Sonny Liston. Everybody thought that this was come-uppance time for Cassius. His behavior became extraordinary. He taunted Liston, whom he dubbed the 'Ugly Bear,' and at the weigh-in he was uncontrollable, almost frenzied, hurling abuse at the champion. His pulse rate rose from his normal 54 to over 120 and his blood pressure soared. The fight doctor said he was unbalanced, and acting like a man in fear for his life. 'Self-induced hysteria,' said Clay's own doctor.

The contest, which was nearly called off because of Clay's condition, took place at the Convention Hall, Miami Beach, on 25 February 1964, and was also extraordinary. Clay boxed on the retreat, flicking out occasional punches, one of which opened a cut under Liston's eye. In the fourth round some of Liston's liniment got into Clay's eyes. In the interval between rounds he began screaming he was blind, and for his gloves to be cut off. He was pushed out for round five and boxed half-blind with his left hand permanently poked out to try to keep Liston at bay.

By the sixth he had recovered, and caught a suddenly weary Liston with some rapid punches. As the seventh was due to start Liston spat out his gumshield. He retired, claiming a shoulder injury. 'I'm the king. I'm the greatest,' Clay screamed at the audience. 'What did I tell you?' he yelled at the press. He danced round the ring, mouth agape, in another display of hysteria.

Clay had been given the belief that he was invincible by the Muslim preacher Malcolm X, later to be assassinated. Clay became a disciple of Elijah Muhammad, Last Messenger of the Lost-Found Nation of Islam, and after the Liston battle assumed his new Black Muslim name of Muhammad Ali.

The champion's return fight with Liston was postponed for six months as Ali underwent an emergency

WORLD HEAVYWEIGHT CHAMPIONSHIP FIGHT · 15 ROUNDS
DIRECT FROM KINSHASA, ZAIRE · TUESDAY, SEPTEMBER 24

GEORGE FOREMAN VS. **MUHAMMAD ALI**

stripped him of his title, and while his argument continued he was out of boxing for over three years.

These might well have proved to be Ali's best years. Because of his amazing speed and footwork – 'float like a butterfly and sting like a bee' – it could be overlooked that he was, in fact, 6 feet 3 inches and some 215 pounds. Apart from freaks like Willard and Carnera there had not been any taller or heavier champions. And Ali was also perfectly proportioned, not tubby like some recent pretenders. Many boxers have punched harder, but Ali was unsurpassed in all other departments of boxing.

Ali was sentenced to five years for refusing induction but in 1970 while on bail pending appeal (eventually successful) he managed to begin a comeback, which led to a world title fight with Joe Frazier, who had been installed as champion in his place. On 8 March 1971, Ali suffered his first defeat, as Joe Frazier outpointed him in New York.

After such a layoff, this was not surprising and many thought it would be the end of an illustrious career. But over the next three years Ali had 14 more bouts. He lost one of them, on points to Ken Norton in San Diego, when he fought for much of the fight with a broken jaw. After less than six months' rest, he avenged this defeat.

On 28 January 1974 he had a tremendous return fight with Frazier in New York, outpointing him and thus avenging both his defeats. Frazier had by then lost his title to George Foreman, the 1968 Olympic champion. Foreman was a devastating puncher, and a man who matched Ali in size and weight, and Ali's next contest was when he challenged him for the title. They fought in Kinshasa, Zaire, on 30 October 1974.

Ali was so confident of his ability to absorb punishment that he sometimes allowed opponents to tire themselves out punching him to the body while he swayed on the ropes (he called it his 'rope-a-dope' trick). He used this ploy against the six-years-younger heavy-punching Foreman, and it worked. Foreman, taken out of his stride and forced to think, became baffled and demoralized, and the amazing Ali knocked him out in the eighth.

He then made ten more successful defenses over the

next three years. The most notable was the third meeting with Frazier, on 1 October 1975, the 'thrilla in Manila.' This was one of the great fights, with both men giving everything, Frazier being the man forced to retire at the end of the fourteenth round. Ali himself sank to the canvas for rest at the verdict, and said that the strain of the fight was the closest thing to death he could imagine.

Nonetheless Ali continued to pursue his career. On 15 February 1978 the 36-year-old boxer was outpointed by a hyped-up Leon Spinks. Spinks was another Olympic gold medalist, and 11½ years younger, but a man little more than a cruiserweight. Ali was lethargic, but the result was still difficult to believe. Ali easily won a return on 15 September 1978 at New Orleans, thus becoming the first to win the title for a third time. Cynics suggested, not in his hearing, that the two bouts with Spinks were engineered to achieve this record.

'The Greatest' retired in June 1979, but emerged from comparative obscurity on 2 October 1980 to challenge the new champion Larry Holmes at Las Vegas, in an ill-advised attempt to win the title for a fourth time. He was now 38, and by his own standards pathetic, and he was forced to retire in the eleventh round. It was the first time he had been stopped.

Soon after Ali's final retirement, there was a marked deterioration in his health. His speech became slurred and he did not move with his usual grace. A form of Parkinson's disease was suspected.

Ali was the most charismatic, outgoing boxer of recent times, a master of his trade. In one moment of euphoria he extended his usual claim: 'I am now the Greatest *of all time*' he said. He was probably right.

Left: Ali's first defeat was in September 1975 against Joe Frazier when Frazier was champion. Frazier (left) tries to catch Ali with a left.

Below far left: Ali regained the title for the second time with this eighth-round knockout of George Foreman in their 'rumble in the jungle' in Kinshasa, Zaire.

Right: Ali slamming a right at the head of Richard Dunn. He knocked out the British challenger in the fifth round at Munich in 1976.

Below left: Throughout his career Ali was the master of whatever situation he was in, be it a fight or an interview. Here he makes a forceful point after his defeat by Holmes.

Below right: Ali on the defensive battles with Larry Holmes in Ali's last title fight which was held in Las Vegas in 1980. The old warrior was stopped for the first time in his career.

Joe Frazier
He stood up to Ali

Joe Frazier was not well equipped for a heavyweight champion. He was just short of 6 feet and although he weighed some 210 pounds a lot of this was in his thick legs. But these legs gave him endless stamina, and he came bobbing forward relentlessly from a crouch that offered taller men only a hard head to hit. Eventually Joe wore his opponents down. He went right to the top, and was the first to beat Ali, in one of three fights with him that were among the best in modern boxing.

Frazier was born on 12 January 1944 in Beaufort, South Carolina, one of 13 children of a very poor family. As a boy his idol was Joe Louis, and he made a punchbag of a sack filled with leaves and dreamed of emulating him. But it was not until he had married at 16 and moved to Philadelphia to work in a slaughterhouse that he took up amateur boxing under trainer 'Yank' Durham.

Right: Joe Frazier in 1973 after beating Bugner.
Below: Frazier took the vacant WBC title by stopping Buster Mathis in the eleventh round at Madison Square Garden, New York, on 4 March 1968.

Left, far left and below left: Smokin' Joe outboxes Jimmy Ellis to become undisputed champion.

Below: Ex-champion Frazier photographed in 1973.

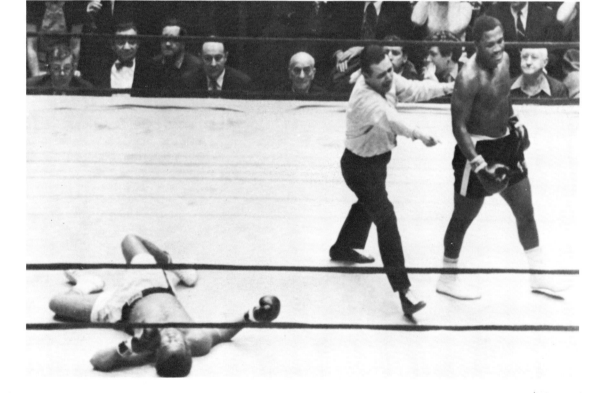

The only boxer to beat him as an amateur was Buster Mathis, twice, but Mathis broke his thumb the second time, allowing Frazier to take an Olympic Games place and win the gold medal in 1964. He turned professional in 1965, and rapidly disposed of a number of opponents.

When Ali was deprived of his title in 1967, the WBA held an eight-man competition to find a new champion. Frazier declined to take part and the WBC matched him with Buster Mathis for their version of the title. They fought in New York on 4 March 1968 and Frazier avenged his old adversary when the referee stopped the fight in the eleventh.

Joe defended his title four times in 1968 and 1969, and then on 16 February 1970 took on the man who had won the WBA competition, Jimmy Ellis, to unify the championship. Joe proved much too strong for the neat-boxing Ellis and nearly knocked him out in the fourth. Ellis was unfit to come out for the fifth, and Joe was undisputed champion.

His style of boring forward, throwing punches without rest, led the ringside scribes to call him the 'Black Marciano' at first, but soon he came to be known as 'Smokin' Joe.' He relaxed between fights singing in one-night stands with a group.

Although Ali was still on the sidelines, he remained the people's choice as champion, whatever the records said, and Ali's eventual comeback inevitably led him to a showdown with Frazier. The fight was in New York on

8 March 1971 and the fans clamored for tickets. It was a classic between the two unbeaten men, with Ali dancing and spearing in punches, Smokin' Joe crowding him to the ropes and belting him about the body. Midway through the last round Joe's best punch, a left hook, dumped Ali on his trunks, and although Ali got up and fought to the bell, Joe had the unanimous verdict. It was Ali's first defeat.

Joe made two more title defenses before meeting another Olympic gold medalist, George Foreman, an unbeaten big puncher, 34 of whose first 37 opponents had failed to hear the final bell. Boxing is largely a question of styles, and Joe's could not cope with Foreman's. At Kingston, Jamaica, on 22 January 1973 Foreman smashed Joe to the floor six times before the referee stopped the fight.

Frazier had a second fight with Ali in 1974 when he was again outpointed in another tremendous battle. Then, when Ali had won the title back from Foreman, they had their third meeting in Manila on 1 October 1975, with the title at stake. This fight swayed back and forth. After ten rounds Ali was on the point of quitting. But it was Frazier who had to give in at last. He took a battering in the fourteenth, and his manager would not let him come out, half-blind, for the final three minutes. Both men were on the point of exhaustion.

Frazier soldiered on for a while, retiring when he lost a second contest with Foreman. Foreman and Ali, twice each, were the only men to beat him. He will be remembered most for his three great fights with Ali. The two men seemed made for each other. In the ballyhoo of their careers Frazier often seemed a helpless butt for Ali's wit, but when the hype and ring hostilities were finally over, Ali praised Frazier highly, and the two became friends.

Joe stayed in boxing, training his sons, one of whom, Marvis, he took to a title shot.

JOE FRAZIER VS. MUHAMMAD ALI

WORLD HEAVYWEIGHT CHAMPIONSHIP

MADISON SQUARE GARDEN / MAR. 8, 1971

Larry Holmes
Nobody likes me

Larry Holmes spent his early career as a champion suffering from the fact that he was not Muhammad Ali. Whoever had succeeded Ali could not help but be in the shadows after the aura which had surrounded the career of 'The Greatest.' Later on, when Larry proved invincible and built up an impressive list of victories, it was said that the opposition was of substandard quality. At the end, when he could have retired with a perfect record, the figures of Rocky Marciano tempted him to take on one fight too many and his record received its first blot. That the public never recognized his talent was one mystery that Holmes did not find elementary.

Holmes was born in Cuthbert, Georgia, on 3 November 1949, one of 11 children. He was not outstanding as an amateur and was 23 before he turned professional in 1973. Despite winning bout after bout he could get no nearer the heavyweight title than sparring with Ali and Joe Frazier. Finally, after winning all his 26 bouts in five years, 22 inside the distance, he was given a chance at the WBC world title.

Leon Spinks, who had won the undisputed title from Ali, was stripped by the WBC for refusing to defend his title against Ken Norton, who was declared champion. When Holmes surprisingly outpointed Norton at Las Vegas on 10 June 1978, the WBC named Holmes as the new champion, although Ali, who later beat Spinks in a return, was clearly the public's choice. Only when Ali announced his retirement was Holmes regarded generally as the new champion. When the WBA perversely recognized John Tate as their champion, the heavyweight title was split again, which, with Muhammad Ali's retirement, contributed to a public loss of interest in the Greatest Prize in Sport.

This was a pity for Holmes, for he proceeded to prove himself a very good champion. From November 1978 to July 1980 he successfully defended seven times, none of the fights going the distance. One of his victims was Mike Weaver, shortly to be WBA champion, so Holmes was clearly the world's best. On 2 October 1980 the ageing Ali tried to prove himself superhuman by winning a version of the heavyweight title for a fourth time, but he was forced to retire in the tenth.

Holmes was proving himself to be a fine boxer with genuine ringcraft, who could take a punch and who could deliver knockout blows with either hand. He continued his winning ways, but his next defense, against Trevor Berbick of Canada, saw him on the canvas before he got up to win on points. Leon Spinks, Ali's one-time conqueror, was then comprehensively beaten in three rounds. After stopping Renaldo Snipes, Holmes faced a much-hyped white hope in Gerry Cooney. But on 12 June 1982, at Las Vegas, Cooney was outclassed and stopped in 13 rounds.

Holmes's next three challengers took him the distance. The last of these, and his hardest opponent so far, was future champion Tim Witherspoon, and Holmes, who boxed defensively, won only on a split decision. But he now claimed an unbeaten record of 43 fights. He disposed quickly of Scott Frank, and was then challenged by Marvis Frazier, son of former champion Joe. Joe and the referee both showed mercy in not allowing Frazier to go beyond the first round.

Sixteen days later Holmes surrendered the WBC title. A new body had been formed called the International Boxing Federation, and it appointed the 34-year-old Holmes as its heavyweight champion. Thus there were shortly three claimants to the heavyweight championship of the world, the candidates of the IBF, WBC and WBA. So far as the public and the fistic fraternity were concerned, the unbeaten Holmes had easily the strongest claim to the championship.

Larry now was beginning to choose less troublesome opponents. He stopped James 'Bonecrusher' Smith and David Bey and was then taken the distance by the lightly regarded Carl Williams.

It was really time for Larry to retire. But he now possessed a record of 48 fights, 48 wins. It was an admirable record but for one thing. The only comparable one was Rocky Marciano's, and his read 49 fights, 49

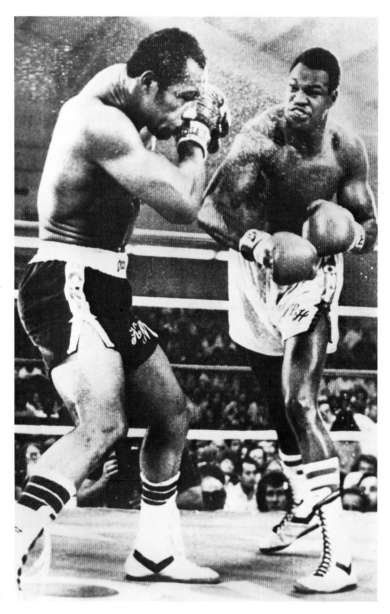

wins. Holmes, still chafing under his lack of acclaim, dearly hoped to equal or beat the record of the very highly acclaimed Rocky, Approaching 36 years old, he did not want to fight any of the young, up-and-coming, dangerous genuine heavyweights. But an acceptable chance arose in a challenge from the light-heavyweight champion, Michael Spinks. Never before had the reigning light-heavy king taken the top crown, although many had tried, and Holmes felt confident of taking Spinks at the Riviera Hotel, Las Vegas, on 20 September 1985. Alas, Larry's ageing legs could not catch up with the dancing Spinks, and Larry lost his title on points – and his unbeaten record.

He announced his retirement, but in 1986 could not resist a second attempt at Spinks. Arriving at Las Vegas Holmes claimed that Nevada boxing judges were often drunk, people got paid off, and he would need a knockout to win. It was an unfortunate outburst, because not only was he forced to apologise by the Nevada State Athletic Commission, but he lost a split decision when most observers thought he had done enough to get the verdict. Holmes filed a protest to the same NSAC, and also to the IBF, and, to show he was not finished, issued a challenge to Cooney, who was planning a comeback.

Holmes was now in his 37th year, having made and invested an estimated $55 million from the ring, as much as anybody except Ali. He owned a beautiful $5 million house, a hotel, a night-club, a restaurant and, at a rough count, 13 cars. He was a proud family man with three children. It was time to enjoy the fruits of his skill and to forget that he had failed to make people like him. At least it seemed they had paid handsomely to see him fight.

Above: Holmes shows his WBC championship belt to the crowd after retaining his title with an eleventh round technical knockout of Earnie Shavers at Las Vegas in 1979.

Left: Larry Holmes (right) lands a blow to the head of Ken Norton, named as champion when Leon Spinks declined to meet him. Holmes went on to take a split decision and the WBC title.

Right: Holmes acknowledges the cheers from the fans as he forces former champion Leon Spinks to retire in the third round at Detroit in 1981.

Mike Tyson
Lost his head over a bird

As the department stores were busy sorting out their Christmas decorations and large-size cash registers in readiness for the 1986 season of goodwill to all men, so Mike Tyson played jingle-bells with Trevor Berbick's senses and announced himself not only the biggest present boxing had been given since Ali but potentially the biggest cash register of all.

The world heavyweight championship at the time was in a sorry state. Holmes had lost his title, but had dealt it a blow before then by aligning himself with the International Boxing Federation, thus forcing the World Boxing Council to find another champion. With the World Boxing Association already proclaiming a champion, there were suddenly three pretenders to the crown, and the confused public was losing interest. In 1986 the champions were, respectively, Michael Spinks, who ended Larry Holmes's long reign, Trevor Berbick, who outpointed Pinklon Thomas, and Tim Witherspoon, who outpointed Tony Tubbs. Apart from these, there were at least another half-dozen active boxers around who had held one or other version of the title. The boxing promoter, Don King, who controlled most of the heavyweight options, began a series of rationalization bouts intended to lead to one undisputed champion in 1987. Tyson's bout with Berbick was one step in this series: the winner was to meet the winner of another bout between Witherspoon and Tubbs, and the winner of *that* would meet Spinks for the unified and genuine world title.

Tyson had come late into this unification series, having been professional only since March 1985, but his claims could not be ignored. He was born in Brooklyn on 30 June 1966 and brought up in Brownsville, a particularly rough neighborhood. Although the boy had the framework for the magnificent physique he developed later, he claims to have been a softie, and much bullied by his companions. It was the killing of one of his pigeons that released the aggression which he had been unconsciously storing up. Pigeons have remained an influence on him and he still keeps some. When he was ten years old and an older boy tore off the head of his pigeon he went wild, beat him up and enjoyed the sensation. At first his new-found power was channelled into bad directions. He became a mugger and thief and, at 13, found himself in a detention center. It is not a new story in the lives of boxers, and neither is that of his salvation. He was pointed toward Cus d'Amato's gym at Catskill, in New York State.

Cus d'Amato was already in his seventies, with a long and distinguished connection with the top echelons of boxing. He had managed Floyd Patterson, the youngest man to win the heavyweight championship, and José Torres, the light-heavyweight champion of the mid-1960s. He began to coach the 13-year-old Tyson, and they developed a relationship which went far beyond that of manager/fighter. Cus d'Amato became Tyson's legal

guardian, and the raw fighter's love for the older man led him to absorb and practice his philosophy – the single-mindedness of purpose, the self-denial, the determination to follow the program to take him to the top.

Tyson also absorbed the boxing lessons. Like Patterson, he is not tall for a heavyweight – some wonder even about the 5 feet 11 inches the record books claim. Among heavyweight champions only Marciano has been shorter than Tyson since Tommy Burns over 80 years ago. Tyson comes weaving in from a crouch, punching upward like Patterson. But there the comparison ends. Whereas Patterson often jumped to punch, Tyson is superbly balanced and punches solidly from a firm footing. He learned from d'Amato where to aim his punches for best effect, and 26 of his first 28 opponents have failed to go the distance.

Tyson's first fight on 6 March 1985 paid a mere $500. He was rarely extended in early bouts, kept busy, and built up a string of rapid knockout victories. After eight months of this career, d'Amato died. Tyson grieved, but the loss made him more determined, if possible, to fulfill d'Amato's ambition for him. He was lucky to have two other mentors to guide him, Jim Jacobs and Bill Cayton. Historian Jacobs has the world's best collection of fight films. Tyson, who watches them, is unusual among boxers in that he knows about old champions. He has a sense of his place in history.

In 1986 Tyson was twice taken the distance, first by James Tillis and then by Mitch Green, both ranked in the top twenty of the WBC ratings. But, in general, the impression he gave was of unstoppable power. Superbly muscled, his most outstanding feature is his 19¾-inch neck; it is almost as if his immense shoulders start just below his ears. As his string of first-round knockouts (15 in 28 fights) mounted, and big men were smashed down with hooks, or lifted off their feet with uppercuts, many opponents began to look apprehensive at the sound of the bell, almost mesmerized into submission.

This led many to think that Tyson had not been properly tested, and that the contest with Berbick, a man of similar physique and an experienced champion with only four defeats, might expose the young challenger's rawness. The fight took place at the Las Vegas Hilton on 22 November 1986.

Berbick's pride forced him to an early downfall. Unwilling to go immediately on the defensive, he made the gesture of taking the fight to Tyson in the first round, a tactic which should at least have had the advantage of surprise. But before the round was over he had been

Left: Mike Tyson, who became the youngest heavyweight champion since Floyd Patterson.
Below: Tyson defiantly wears the black trunks traditionally allowed the champion while Berbick retaliates with long black socks. Tyson won in the second at Las Vegas in 1986.

staggered by a left hook to the body, been unable to avoid more punishment, and found it already too late to change his tactics. In the second round another left hook knocked him to the canvas. He took the eight count standing and looking belligerent, but neither Tyson nor the crowd was fooled. After a few more solid punches, a left high on Berbick's head brought the end. Berbick momentarily froze, Tyson pushed him away from the clinch, and Berbick reeled backward and fell as the blow took effect. He groped his way up, reeled across the ring, fell, rose, and reeled back again, like a child learning to walk in a playpen. The referee stopped the fight, commenting later 'Everything he'd got had "good night" written all over it.'

Tyson had won in 2 minutes 35 seconds of the second round – by far his most impressive performance to date. He looked every inch a real champion, a man destined to give the heavyweight division its dignity again. He was WBC title-holder, at 20 years and 5 months the youngest of all heavyweight champions. Still self-possessed, he announced his intention to be the oldest, too. He had just over 28 years to go.

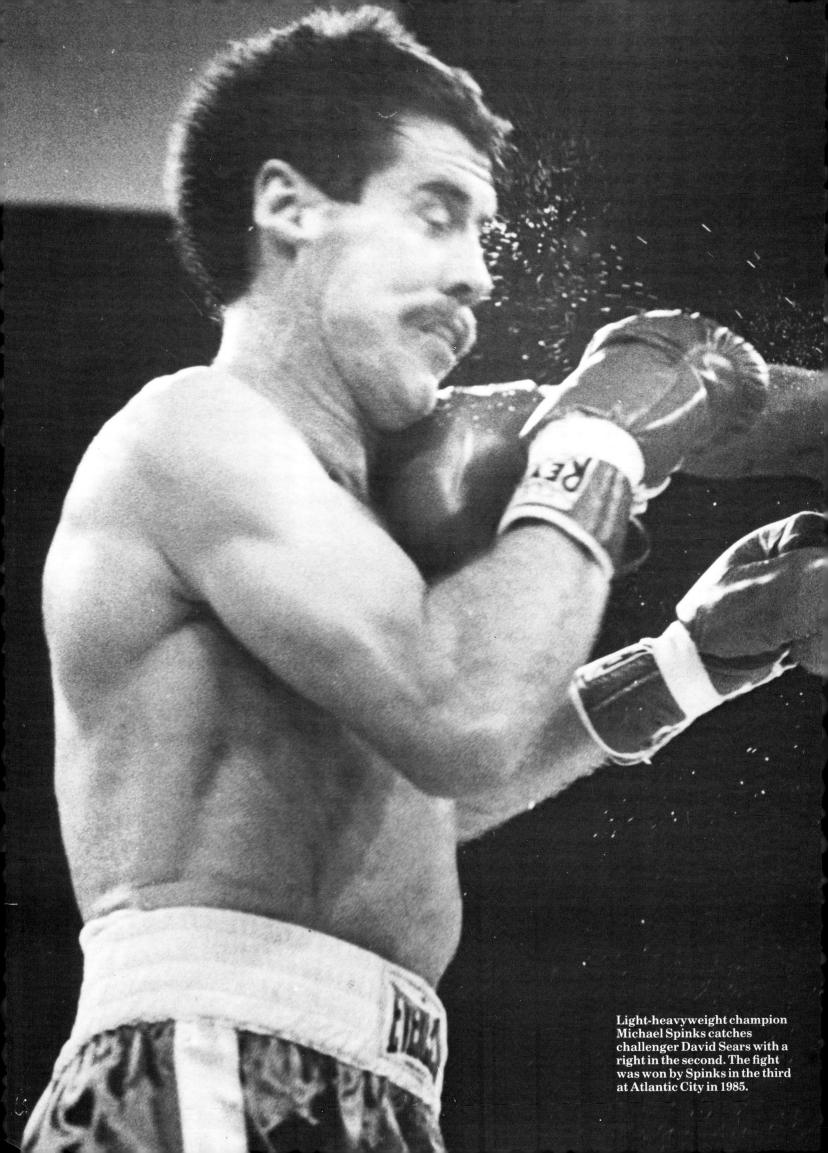

Light-heavyweight champion Michael Spinks catches challenger David Sears with a right in the second. The fight was won by Spinks in the third at Atlantic City in 1985.

Light- heavyweight

Georges Carpentier
A show-business profile

Georges Carpentier was a boxing genius, a man who began professionally at 14 years old, and boxed his way up the weights until he fought for the heavyweight championship of the world. On the way he won national, European and world titles. He was also extraordinarily handsome, with a film-star profile. When war came he was decorated for gallantry. In fact, 'Gorgeous Georges' was almost too good to be true. He not only made boxing popular in France, but noticeably drew more women to the ringside. Not for him the usual Battling Bomber type of nickname. Georges was the 'Orchid Man.'

Carpentier was born on 12 January 1894 in Lens, France, the son of a miner. At 10 years old he joined the Regeneratrice Gymnastic Society in Lens and first appeared in a ring aged 12, practicing French boxing, or 'savate,' in which the feet are used.

Right: Georges Carpentier, the Frenchman who took the world light-heavyweight title.

Center right, above: Carpentier photographed while serving in the air force during the First World War. He was decorated for his gallantry.

Center right, below: Carpentier (dark shorts) boxing Bombardier Billy Wells in 1913. Carpentier twice knocked out the British champion for the European heavyweight title.

Far right: Gunboat Smith gets a left to Carpentier's jaw in 1914, but Carpentier won to become 'white heavyweight champion' of the world.

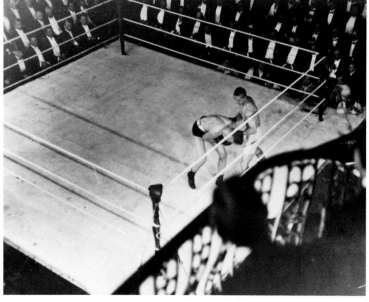

Above: Carpentier knocked out Britain's Joe Beckett in the first round at Holborn, London in 1919.
Left: The Orchid Man enjoyed a wide following outside the fight game, and on his retirement appeared in variety.
Right: Georges leaving the ring after he surprisingly lost his world light-heavyweight title to Battling Siki in Paris in 1922.

He teamed up with François Descamps, a man who travelled France with a one-man show. When they saw *la boxe Anglaise* Georges took to it, and on 1 November 1908 had his first match, at Maisons-Lafitte, against an English boy called Salmon, whom he beat. By 15 June 1911, the 17-year-old Georges, who had had 50 fights in the meantime, was welterweight champion of France.

The same year, on 23 October, Georges was in London to beat Young Joseph, who retired in the tenth round, leaving Georges the first Frenchman to be a European champion (and still the youngest ever European champion at any weight). Four months later in Monaco he knocked out British titleholder Jim Sullivan in the second to become the European middleweight champion.

He was only 19, and still gaining weight, when he challenged Bombardier Billy Wells, the British heavyweight champion, for the European title. At the Ghent Exhibition on 1 June 1913, he recovered from a first-round knockdown to knock Wells out in the fourth.

Wells himself was a lady-pleaser (he was called 'Beautiful Billy') and this match and the return at the National Sporting Club in London caused anxiety in many feminine hearts. Georges won the return in a sensational 73 seconds, including the count.

While Jack Johnson was still heavyweight champion of the world, an unofficial 'white championship' was promoted. On 14 July 1914 Georges met the American 'holder' of this title, Ed 'Gunboat' Smith, in London. When Georges slipped in the sixth, and the Gunboat cuffed him while he was down, Georges was given the 'title' on a disqualification, the last man to hold it.

Nineteen days later war broke out and Carpentier became an officer in the air force, where he was decorated with the *Croix de Guerre* and the *Médaille Militaire*. Georges lost five years of his prime, but in 1919 quickly proved himself to be still the scourge of British heavyweights by dispatching Dick Smith and then the champion, Joe Beckett, in a sensational 74 seconds in London.

The great American promoter Tex Rickard had the idea of putting the debonair war hero from France against the crude, unshaven world champion, Jack Dempsey, who had noticeably not found time to enlist. It must be remembered, however, that despite his one-man humiliation of British heavyweights, Carpentier was all this time never more than a light-heavyweight. To make the Dempsey fight more appealing, Carpentier went to America and won the world light-heavyweight title by knocking out Battling Levinsky in four rounds at Jersey City. Rickard publicized the Dempsey-Carpentier contest as the 'Battle of the Century' and it provoked enormous enthusiasm, the receipts of $1,789,238 being the first to exceed $1 million.

Carpentier was a brilliant boxer with a swift and devastating right, which, landing on an opponent's chin, usually meant curtains. But he broke his right thumb hitting Dempsey in the second round, and could not withstand the power of the heavier man thereafter, being knocked out in the fourth.

Georges was not quite so good after this. He lost his world title surprisingly to the raw Battling Siki in Paris in 1922, and returned to America to lose to Gene Tunney. He finally retired in 1927 to open a bar in Paris. He remained a celebrity until his death in Paris in 1975.

Michael Spinks
Maker of records

In the 1976 Olympic Games in Montreal, 20-year-old Michael Spinks reached the middleweight boxing final with only two bouts – there had been a bye and two forfeits in his early rounds. He fought Rufat Riskiev, of the USSR, the world amateur champion who had beaten him six months previously in Tashkent. Riskiev spent two rounds piling up the points, but in the third Spinks caught him such a blow in the stomach that Riskiev doubled up in pain and the referee was forced to stop the fight and award it to Spinks.

In the next final, the light-heavyweight, Spinks's older brother, Leon, fought Sixto Soria, of Cuba, a knock-out specialist who had dispatched three previous opponents in a total of 9 minutes 5 seconds. But it was Spinks who threw all the painful leather in a rough fight, knocking Soria down in the first and forcing the referee to call a halt in the third. It was the first time brothers had won Olympic gold medals in boxing. This was not to be the

Below: Spinks (left) attacks Larry Holmes in the 1985 fight which gave Spinks the IBF heavyweight crown.

only boxing record for the Spinks boys. Three more were to come in the professional heavyweight ranks.

The boys were born in St Louis, Missouri, almost exactly three years apart – Leon on 11 July 1953, then Michael on 13 July 1956. Both were good amateur boxers. Leon won three American titles, losing only eight of 127 contests. Michael was Golden Gloves light-middleweight champion in 1974 and middleweight champion in 1976.

Leon turned professional in January 1977 – Michael was only three months behind him. On 15 February 1978 Leon caused one of the biggest upsets in modern boxing when he outpointed Muhammad Ali for the undisputed heavyweight championship of the world. It was only his eighth professional fight – nobody had won it more quickly. He reigned for only seven months, however, Ali outpointing him in the guaranteed return. Leon later fought Larry Holmes, the WBC heavyweight champion, but was badly beaten by the third. At less than 200 pounds, he was not a true heavyweight, and later won the North American Boxing Federation cruiserweight title.

Michael, at 6 feet 2 inches, was tall and slim for his class, which turned out to be the light-heavyweights. After winning his first 16 professional fights he was given a chance to win the WBA light-heavyweight title against champion Eddie Mustaffa Muhammad at Las Vegas on 18 July 1981. Michael outpointed his man in a smooth performance.

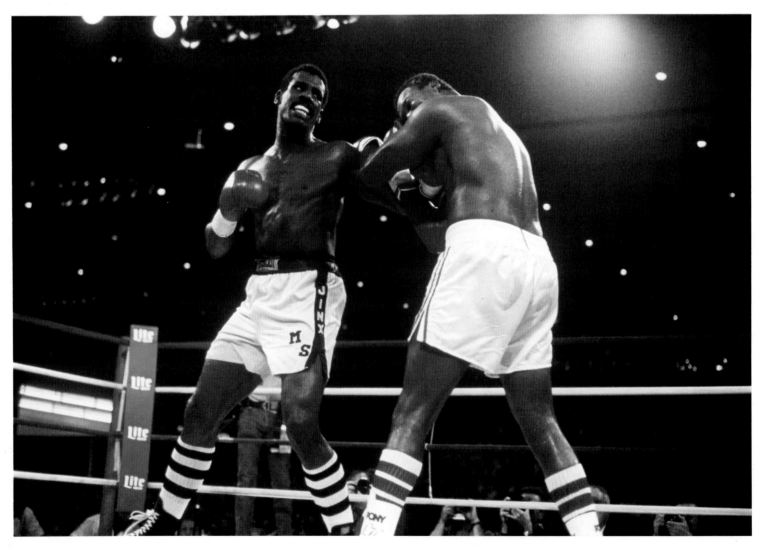

Above: Vonzell Johnson forces Michael Spinks to cover up during the light-heavyweight title fight at Atlantic City in 1981. Spinks knocked Johnson out in the seventh.
Right: After winning the IBF heavyweight belt (round his waist), Spinks gave up his three light-heavyweight belts.

Fast, with a long reach and good footwork, and carrying a punch capable of knocking out an opponent suitably softened up, Spinks had little trouble in ruling his division. In November 1981 he knocked out Vonzell Johnson in the seventh; in February 1982 the referee came to the assistance of Mustapha Wasajji of Uganda in the sixth; in April Murray Sutherland was knocked out in the eighth; in June Jerry Celestine was stopped in the eighth; in September Johnny Davis was knocked out in the ninth; and then on 19 March 1983 Spinks took on the WBC champion, Dwight Muhammad Qawi (formerly Dwight Braxton), to unify the title. Qawi put up the best resistance yet, but Spinks outpointed him over 15 rounds to become undisputed light-heavyweight champion of the world. All these bouts were in Atlantic City.

Spinks then boxed in Vancouver to dispose of Oscar Rivadeneyra, saved by the referee in the tenth, before returning to Atlantic City to outpoint Eddie Davis over 12 rounds, and force the referee to rescue David Sears in the third. On 6 June 1985 Spinks made his last defense of the title, the referee deciding Jim McDonald had taken enough punishment in the eighth at Las Vegas.

Spinks then challenged Larry Holmes for the IBF heavyweight crown. Both boxers were unbeaten, but whereas Holmes was a natural heavyweight, Spinks went on a 4500-calories-a-day diet to add 25 pounds to his normal 175 pound fighting weight. His incentive was a payday of over $1 million, far more than he was being paid to defend his light-heavyweight title. His advantage was that he was at his peak, while Holmes was an ageing giant prolonging his career in an attempt to equal Marciano's record of 49 straight wins. Even so, Holmes was a 3-1 favorite for the eagerly awaited fight.

In the event the 11,000 at the Riviera Hotel in Las Vegas found the blown-up Spinks still fast enough and skillful enough to keep the 35-year-old Holmes at bay. Larry's legs not only could not catch up with Spinks but also could not take him out of trouble later in the fight when Michael darted in with plenty of overhand rights of his own. Spinks was given a unanimous points verdict.

Michael was stripped by both the WBA and WBC of his light-heavyweight titles for taking the IBF title, but he had set up two more records for the Spinks family. He had not only avenged brother Leon's bad defeat by Holmes, but they had become the only brothers to hold a version of the heavyweight crown. Previously Max and Buddy Baer had been the only brothers to fight for it, but only Max won it. Also Michael had become the first reigning light-heavyweight champ to take the heavyweight title: Jack Root, Philadelphia Jack O'Brien, Georges Carpentier, Tommy Loughran, John Henry Lewis, Billy Conn, Joey Maxim, Gus Lesnevich, Archie Moore and Bob Foster had all tried and failed.

In a return on 19 April 1986 Spinks again beat Holmes on points in Las Vegas, but this time it was a very controversial split decision, with most neutrals thinking Holmes had won. However, Spinks was still champion, and the name Spinks was already of unique significance in the history of the fight game.

Randolph Turpin (left)
flattens the face of Charles
Humez in defending his
European middleweight title
in London in 1953.

Middleweight

Tony Zale
The Man of Steel

Fight followers could be almost sure of a feast when Tony Zale was boxing. He knew only one way to fight: on the offensive and punching. It was a technique which left him open to a good deal of punishment himself, but he could take it, so his battles were usually all-action affairs. The three with Rocky Graziano have become classics of the ring.

Zale was born Anthony Florian Zaleski on 29 May 1913 in Gary, Indiana, of Polish parents. He worked in the steel mills and boxed as an amateur, winning most of his bouts, many inside the distance.

At 21, he turned professional, but was too ambitious. Fighting every fortnight or so he lost his sharpness and enthusiasm, and after a year he went back to the steel mills. Two years later he tried again, and, with Sam Pian and Art Winch managing him, made steady progress up the rankings. He was called the 'Man of Steel,' which reflected his style as well as his origins. Eventually he outpointed Al Hostak, the National Boxing Association middleweight champion, in an overweight bout, which earned him a title shot. He won it by knocking out Hostak in the thirteenth round on 19 July 1940 in Seattle. In a return on 28 May 1941 at Chicago, Zale delivered the knockout in the second.

The New York Commission version of the crown became vacant, and Georgie Abrams was named to face Zale. When Tony took a 15-round decision at Madison Square Garden, New York, on 28 November 1941, there was an undisputed middleweight champion for the first time in ten years.

After service in the navy during the war, and a five-year layoff, Zale resumed his career and was soon challenged by a man nine years younger, who was building a big reputation with some all-action aggressive displays. His name was Rocky Graziano, and the two met on 27 September 1946 at Yankee Stadium in New York. It was a terrific battle from the first bell, with Graziano down within a minute but coming back strongly to have Zale groggy at the end of the round. In the second Zale was down after a tremendous barrage, and appeared on the verge of being knocked out when the bell intervened. But he survived the third, fourth and fifth rounds, despite a badly damaged nose which made it difficult to breathe. In the sixth, as Zale stood dazed and apparently ready for the kill, he threw a last desperate right to Graziano's solar plexus, and as Graziano stood ashen knocked him out with a left hook.

There was a clamor for a return, and 18,547 spectators, an indoor record, piled into the Chicago Stadium on 16 July 1947. This fight was the opposite of the first. Zale outboxed Graziano and battered him for four rounds. But in the fifth Graziano fought like a wild man, and in the sixth Zale was helpless when the referee stepped in and awarded Graziano the championship.

These fights caused such excitement that a decider was a natural. It took place at Newark, New Jersey, on 10 June 1948. Of these two terribly tough men, Tony Zale, the Man of Steel, proved to have lasted the course better. Despite Graziano's efforts, Zale punched harder and floored him in the third, then knocked his man completely unconscious with a right to the body and a left to the jaw. Zale had regained the middleweight title.

Tony was now 35, and possibly underestimated the draining power of these three fights and the strength of his next challenger, Marcel Cerdan of France. At Roosevelt Stadium, only three months after the Graziano fight, Zale was unable to come out for the twelfth round after a sound beating. The Man of Steel retired. His series with Graziano will never be forgotten.

Right: Tony Zale is hugged by co-manager Art Winch while Rocky Graziano is revived after their rubber match at Newark, New Jersey in 1948.

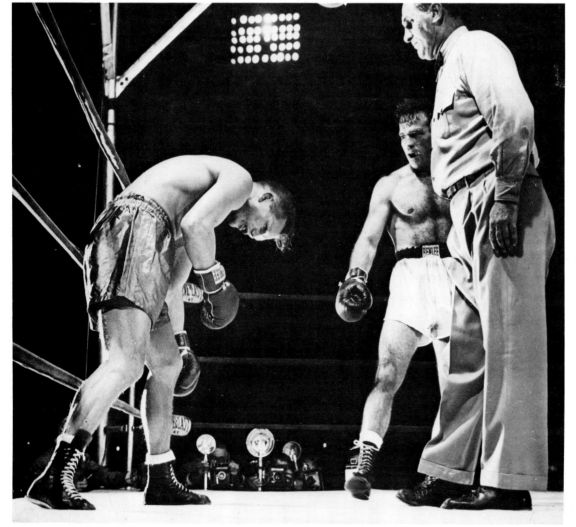

Above: Tony Zale, of Gary, Indiana, a compact hard-hitting middleweight champion of the world.

Above left: Graziano lies slumped on the canvas after a punch from Zale in the first of their outstanding fights for the middleweight title.

Left: In an era of great middleweights, Zale had no sooner seen off the fierce challenge of Rocky Graziano than he was defending against another great champion, Marcel Cerdan. Zale sags to the canvas as his title passes to the Frenchman at Jersey City on 21 September 1948.

Rocky Graziano
Somebody up there likes me

Rocky Graziano's career was one of those rags to riches, bad to good, stories of which boxing boasts so many examples. From reform school and prison, and being kicked out of the army, to championship of the world and television personality: he could hardly have expected life to treat him so well. No wonder they made a film of it, and no wonder it was called *Somebody Up There Likes Me*.

Rocky was born in New York on 1 January 1922. His real name is Thomas Rocco Barbella. He had a tough East Side upbringing, running wild with gangs from schooldays, stealing from cars and apartments. Eventually he was sent to reform school for breaking open slot machines, then in prison where he assaulted a guard.

A rugged street fighter, he began professional boxing on 31 March 1942, and then was drafted into the army. Discipline was no good for Rocky. He punched an officer and fled, managing to get in a few more ring fights before the military police caught up with him. The army soon decided they did not want him and he was given a dishonorable discharge.

Resuming his ring career, he was very busy, usually knocking out his opponents but occasionally dropping a decision to a clever boxer. Rocky's style was simple. He was very tough, and he threw punches from all angles, many of them swings and swipes not to be found in the textbooks. If one landed, his opponent usually wobbled, and then he was merciless. He was a natural middleweight, one of the toughest of all divisions.

Rocky's career took an upswing when he scored a surprise third round knockout of the highly rated Billy Arnold. Promoters and public liked his style. Twice, in overweight matches, he knocked out the world welterweight champion, Freddie Cochrane, both times in the tenth round. He then avenged two defeats by Harold Green by beating him comprehensively in three. He destroyed Marty Servo, the new welterweight king, in two rounds in another overweight match. Servo, whose nose was broken, did not fight again.

All this led to his challenge to Tony Zale for the middleweight crown on 27 September 1946. The explosive Rocky was expected to win, and having knocked Zale down in the second piled in enough punishment to destroy any but the Man of Steel. But in the sixth Graziano was paralyzed with a solar plexus shot and knocked out. 'The count crept up on me,' he said. When he got his breath back he threw himself furiously at Zale, wanting to continue the fight.

Rocky trained to perfection for the return, and on the principle that the winner would be the man who got his really explosive punch in first, he concentrated on this objective. Zale took the early rounds, but Rocky got in as planned in the fifth. In the sixth he had Zale draped over the middle rope as he tore into him, and the referee intervened. Rocky's fierce fighting had earned him the middleweight championship of the world.

Rocky lost his title to Zale on 10 June 1948. Rocky appeared to have lost a lot of his sting, and Zale regained the championship with a third round knockout.

Graziano's criminal record did not help him later in the year. There had been rumors of a fix before the Servo fight and then Rocky was found not to have reported an attempt to bribe him before a fight with Reuben Shank, which in the event was called off when Rocky injured himself. Rocky was questioned for 15 hours in the DA's office and suspended for a year from boxing in New York.

On his return Rocky was undefeated for three years, and challenged Sugar Ray Robinson in another attempt on the middleweight title on 16 April 1952 in Chicago. He put the great Sugar Ray down, but was knocked out in the third. He retired, but accepted one more fight, losing a decision to Chuck Davey.

In 1953 Rocky was invited onto a Martha Raye television show, and so delighted audiences with his humorous talk that he became a TV celebrity for a while. His autobiography *Somebody Up There Likes Me* was filmed with Paul Newman playing Rocky. Meanwhile the delinquent from the East Side took over a smart New York restaurant. The fight game had been kind to Rocky.

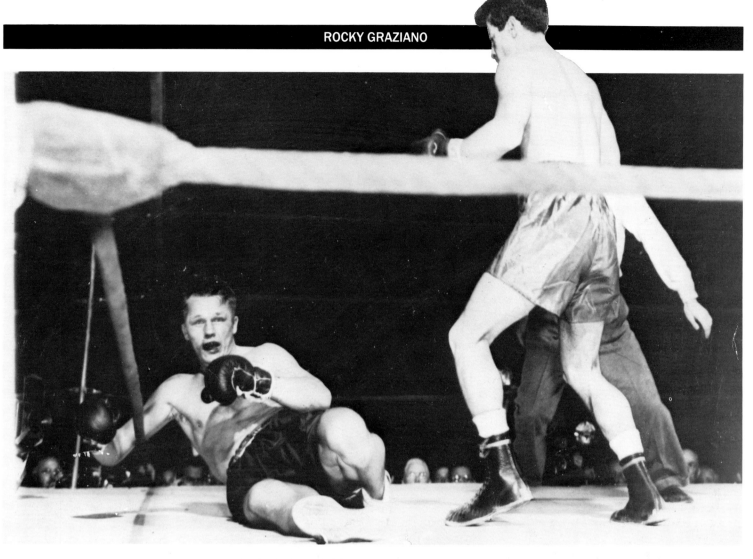

Above: One of Rocky Graziano's successful moments in the saga with Tony Zale. This is the first of their three gruelling battles, and Zale is subsiding by the ropes. Rocky won the second of their fights to become world champion.

Left: An intense-looking Rocky Graziano, with personalized headguard, in training. The manner of his boxing, more scrapping than noble art, led to exciting battles which drew the fans. His down-to-earth style impressed television viewers, too.

Right: Zale starts for a neutral corner as Rocky lies motionless on the canvas. The fight, which took place on 10 June 1948 at Newark, New Jersey, cost Rocky his title.

Marcel Cerdan
An empty chair

Marcel Cerdan was one of the great middleweights, but his career was cut short just as he was about to reap his full reward. Even so, his record is outstanding.

Cerdan, whose first name was really Marcellin, was born in Sidi-bel-Abbes, Algeria, on 22 July 1916, the fourth son of a butcher. At 17 he turned professional. When he was 22 he became French welterweight champion, outpointing Omar Konidri in Casablanca, and on 3 June 1939 he beat Salverio Turiello of Italy in Milan to become European champion. Soon he was to serve in the French army until the fall of France in 1940.

By 1945 he was a middleweight, and he took the French title with a third round knockout of Assane Diouf in Paris on 30 November, and followed this on 2 February 1946 with the European championship, when he knocked out Léon Fouquet of Belgium.

Another Belgian, Cyrille Delannoit, spoiled his record by outpointing him narrowly in Brussels in 1948 but less than two months later he easily reversed the decision by regaining his title.

He had now been a French champion for ten years and a European champion for nine, and between defenses had been making trips to the United States to record more victories. Cerdan was a true fighter, without a weakness. He had strength, skill and stamina, he could take a punch, and he possessed a knockout punch himself. In the early 1940s he had not been a bad soccer player either, being selected for the Moroccan team.

On 21 September 1948 he got his chance at the world title, challenging Tony Zale at Jersey City. In the third round his right hand was injured, and he fought the knockout specialist Zale with one good hand. Marcel dominated the fight, and in the eleventh feinted with his right and shook Zale with a left hook to the chin. Two more lefts and Zale was down, to be saved by the bell. But he could not come out for the twelfth and Marcel was the world champion.

Zale retired, and Marcel's first defense was against Jake LaMotta at Detroit on 16 June 1949. Once again Cerdan was forced to fight under a handicap. He pulled a muscle in his shoulder in the first round. LaMotta was too tough to beat with one hand, but Marcel stayed in the fight for nine rounds, finally being unable to come out for the tenth. It was only his fourth defeat in 123 fights – the two noted above, and two dubious disqualifications.

Cerdan lived only for the chance of revenge the return clause gave him. He and his manager were on a Constellation airliner bound for New York to reclaim his crown when the plane crashed into a mountain in the Azores. All aboard were killed. Marcel Cerdan, the idol of France, was nationally mourned. At the Montmartre café that he used in Paris, an empty chair remains against the wall in his memory.

Left: Marcel Cerdan (left) in action against Cyrille Delannoit in their European middleweight championship fight in 1948. Delannoit inflicted Marcel's first defeat in over 100 contests, but Marcel regained the title in the return.

Above right: Cerdan finds the face of Tony Zale with a hard right in their 1948 world title bout at the Roosevelt Stadium, Jersey City. Zale was unable to continue after severe punishment in the eleventh round and Cerdan was crowned king.

Right: Marcel Cerdan, sporting a black eye after his title victory, escorts the famous French music hall singer, Edith Piaf (left) and Simone Cartier to the Versailles night-club, New York, the day after his win.

Far right: Marcel relaxes with a copy of the New York *Daily News* which reports his successful title fight. The photograph in the newspaper appears on page 69 of this book.

Jake LaMotta
The Raging Bull

Few fighters came tougher than Jake LaMotta. He traded leather with the world's best, including Sugar Ray Robinson six times, and fought in some of the bloodiest battles, but few ever stopped him. His non-stop attacking methods earned him the nickname of the 'Bronx Bull.'

LaMotta was born on 10 July 1921 on the Lower East Side of New York City, but lived most of his fighting life in the Bronx. Son of an Italian father and Jewish mother, his real name was Giacobe LaMotta. He was a thief and general delinquent as a boy, ending up in the same reform school as Rocky Graziano, where he took up boxing. He claimed to have had a thousand street fights and a thousand amateur bouts.

As an amateur he won a Diamond Belt championship, and turned professional shortly before turning 20. He

Above: Jake LaMotta, tearful after his 1949 victory over Marcel Cerdan. With him (left to right) are former heavyweight champion Joe Louis, trainer Al Silvani and brother Joey.

Right: Jake LaMotta, nicknamed the 'Bronx Bull' for his relentless punching technique.

lost twice in his first year or so, once to Sugar Ray Robinson, and then, on 5 February 1943, he gave Sugar Ray his first defeat, knocking him through the ropes on his way to a points win. Robinson reversed the decision three weeks later and beat LaMotta three more times. Campaigning as a middleweight Jake also lost to former welterweight champion Fritzie Zivic, but beat him three times. He also campaigned successfully among the light-heavies and heavyweights.

LaMotta did not have a manager, although his brother helped with his affairs. Although he was beating all the main contenders, he found it impossible to secure a title fight. On 14 November 1947 he lost to Billy Fox in New York, the referee stopping the contest in the fourth round. There were strong suspicions that this fight had been fixed for betting purposes, and many years later LaMotta admitted before the Senate investigation this

Below: Tiberio Mitri of Italy receives a long left from LaMotta. Mitri was unsuccessful in this 1950 challenge for the world title.

was so, claiming it was necessary to lose to enable him to get a chance for a title fight later on.

This came on 16 June 1949, when he challenged Marcel Cerdan, the French holder. Cerdan was a rough two-fisted fighter like LaMotta, and the match was a tough one, with Cerdan retiring after ten rounds claiming an injured shoulder.

LaMotta outpointed Tiberio Mitri of Italy in his first defense, then had his most exciting victory defending against Laurent Dauthuille, at Detroit on 13 September 1950. The Frenchman had already outpointed Jake the year before, and was well on the way to doing so again. LaMotta was taking punishment in the last round, well behind on points, when he suddenly caught Dauthuille with a tremendous punch. Jake followed up and knocked his man out with 13 seconds left.

LaMotta was now challenged by Sugar Ray Robinson, their sixth meeting. The fight was in Chicago on 14 February 1951, and was a tough one, with Sugar Ray's skillful boxing generally on top of LaMotta's battering ram tactics, and eventually a strong rally by Jake ended when Robinson punched him to a standstill in the thirteenth, the referee coming to Jake's rescue.

Above: Sugar Ray Robinson (left) was an unfortunate contemporary for LaMotta. Robinson won five of their six encounters. This shot is from their sixth fight in Chicago in 1951, when Robinson took Jake's middleweight crown.

After a few more losses over the next three years, Jake decided to retire. Throughout his career he had had problems with his weight, often putting on 20 or 30 pounds between fights. He should, perhaps, have been a light-heavyweight, but the middleweight division was the rich and glamorous one.

Perhaps because of his weight problems, LaMotta was an edgy and sometimes violent man in private life. On retirement he took a night-club in Miami Beach, where he drank heavily, and his second wife and children left him. There was trouble with a 14-year-old girl, and LaMotta returned to New York and entered show business, making appearances in films, giving talks and playing host at a topless night-club. 'An Evening with Jake LaMotta' included a recital of the 'contender' speech from the film *On the Waterfront*. Jake's autobiography, *Raging Bull*, was itself made into a very successful film starring Robert De Niro as LaMotta.

Sugar Ray Robinson

Five times the champion

Robinson is often summed up by boxing writers as the best pound-for-pound boxer of all time. Although he fought for 25 years in the top class, with over 200 fights, at the end of his career his face was as handsome and unmarked as when he had started. In his prime 'Sugar Ray' had 91 fights without a defeat, winning the welterweight championship of the world in 1946, and the middleweight championship an unprecedented five times. He was all but world champion at three weights.

Sugar Ray was born Walker Smith on 3 May 1921 in Detroit, Michigan. When he was 12 his parents separated, and the young Smith went with his mother to New York where he ran the streets until a priest took him to a gymnasium run by trainer George Gainsford. Sugar Ray made his amateur debut standing in for a boy who had been passed as unfit, taking the boy's card and identity and boxing as 'Ray Robinson.' It was a ring name he decided to keep. Robinson went on to win a Golden Gloves Championship and turned professional in 1940. He quickly ran up a string of victories. When somebody commented to Gainsford that he had a sweet boxer, Gainsford replied Robinson was 'As sweet as sugar.' The description stuck.

Sugar Ray met his first defeat in Detroit in 1943 after 40 wins. Jake LaMotta, whom he had recently outpointed, got on top of him in a hard fight and outpointed him. This was Sugar Ray's last defeat for eight years.

Because of the war he had to wait until 1946 for his first chance to win a world title. In New York on 20 December he outpointed Tommy Bell to become the welterweight champion.

Over the next four years, Sugar Ray defended this title five times and then challenged for the middleweight crown. This was held by Jake LaMotta whom Robinson had beaten three times since that only blot on his record eight years earlier. In Chicago, on 14 February 1951, Sugar Ray put on a brilliant display of boxing which flummoxed the tough 'Bronx Bull' so completely that the referee had to come to the rescue of the middleweight champion in the thirteenth round.

Sugar Ray gave up his welter crown to rule the middleweights. He was proving to be a brilliant boxer-fighter, completely dedicated to his craft. Not only had he learned the skills of boxing, he had also studied anatomy so that he could make his punches tell.

Outside the ring he was also a colorful character with numerous small family businesses in Harlem and an entourage of helpers and followers. On winning the middleweight crown, Robinson decided on a holiday tour of Europe. He would pay for his expensive lifestyle by knocking over the leading middleweights. The press made great fun of what they called the circus surrounding the champ's pink Cadillac: it included not only sisters, manager and wife, trainers and secretary, but golf partner, dwarf mascot and even hairdresser.

Robinson won according to plan in Paris, Zurich, Antwerp, Liège, Berlin and Turin, but bit off more than he could chew in London, where the brilliant British and European champion Randy Turpin ended his eight-year 91-fight run without defeat by outpointing him and taking the title.

Above: Sugar Ray Robinson, the center of attention in Paris traffic in 1951.

Left: The end of a roundhouse swing aimed by Robinson at Carl 'Bobo' Olson in their 1952 world title bout.

Right: A distressed Robinson, suffering from heat exhaustion, in the thirteenth round of his 1952 challenge for Joey Maxim's light-heavyweight crown.

Top and above: Sugar Ray goes through the ropes in his world title fight with Gene Fullmer in 1957. He climbed back, but lost on points over 15 rounds.

Right: Robinson in his Cadillac, much admired for its pink color, arrives with his entourage at a Paris gym.

Sixty-four days later, on 12 September 1951, there was a return at the Polo Grounds in New York, and Robinson showed his courage by coming back from the brink of defeat. In the tenth round, despite a bad cut near his left eye, he suddenly launched an assault on Turpin which forced the referee to step in to save the Englishman, and Robinson had regained his crown.

Having beaten future and past champions in Carl Olson and Rocky Graziano, Robinson challenged for the light-heavyweight title. As a boy his heroes had been Joe Louis, whose bag he had carried to the gym, and Henry Armstrong. Armstrong had been world champion at three weights, and in an attempt to emulate him Sugar Ray stepped into the ring at the Yankee Stadium on 25 June 1952 to face champion Joey Maxim.

Robinson was giving away 14 pounds, but completely outboxed his opponent and must have won but for one thing – it was the hottest day of the year at 104 deg F (40 deg C). Referee Ruby Goldstein was forced to give up after 10 rounds, and Robinson himself was too exhausted to box on after 13 rounds.

On 18 December 1952 Robinson announced his retirement. He began dancing in a cabaret act, but income tax demands and a hankering for the ring caused him to make a comeback in 1955. He was in his 35th year, and lost his second warm-up fight, at which Gainsford and trainer Wiley left him. But they returned when he astonishingly reached championship class again.

On 9 December 1955 Robinson knocked out Carl 'Bobo' Olson in the second round in Chicago to regain the middleweight title that he had relinquished unbeaten. He beat Olson again, and then lost his title on points to Gene Fullmer in New York, after being knocked out of the ring. Amazingly, back in Chicago, Sugar Ray knocked out Fullmer in the fifth round to win the title for the fourth time. On 23 September 1957 in New York he lost on points in a tremendous battle with Carmen Basilio, in which both men were battered and needed great courage to last the 15 rounds. Again, back in Chicago on 25 March 1958, Sugar Ray regained the title with a points win. His record of winning the crown five times is unlikely ever to be surpassed.

On 22 January 1960 Robinson's world championship reign finally came to an end when Paul Pender outpointed him in Boston. Robinson was nearly 39 years old. He failed to regain the title in a re-match in June. Next he challenged Gene Fullmer who was recognized as champion by the NBA. Sugar Ray drew with him over 15 rounds at Los Angeles. In a second attempt to win this title, on 4 March 1961, he was outpointed at Las Vegas in the last of his 22 world title bouts.

Robinson decided to carry on boxing, a decision which caused his wife to leave him, as had happened to his idol Joe Louis. He finally retired in his 45th year in 1965. Although he lost a few fights in those last four years heat exhaustion was the only opponent ever to stop him.

Randolph Turpin
Too many women

Randolph Turpin was probably the best British boxer since the Second World War. When, at only 23 years old, he inflicted on the great Sugar Ray Robinson his first defeat in eight years, it appeared that he was about to become one of the all-time giants of the ring. But Randolph could not handle fame, and the glory drifted away and was replaced by tragedy.

Randolph Turpin was born in Leamington on 7 June 1928 to a black father and white mother. His father, who had been gassed in the war, died when Randy was nine months old, leaving Mrs Turpin to raise her three boys and two girls in hard times.

Randy suffered from bronchitis as a child, and his determination to make himself strong took him to a health fanatic who helped him build up his body. At 12 he was boxing at Leamington Boys Club where he was taken on by George Middleton, a local trainer.

Randy was something of a bully as a child, and when he married at 18, his wife left him within a year and sued him for assault. Randy, a cook in the navy, had by then made a highly promising impression as an amateur boxer, winning the ABA welter and middleweight titles at 17 and 18 years old. He turned professional and beat Vince Hawkins, the British middleweight champion, when he was officially still too young to challenge for the title. But what was to be a pattern in Randolph's career

Above: Randolph Turpin in training three months before he became world champion. Turpin was a brilliant champion, at his peak the equal of Sugar Ray Robinson, but he could not organize his life outside the ring and was denied the long reign at the top that his talents merited.

Left: Turpin beats Robinson to the punch with a long left in his world-title-winning fight at Earls Court, London on 10 July 1951. Sugar Ray was easily outpointed in Turpin's best performance in the ring.

first manifested itself when he fought Jean Stock, of France. Just before the fight he heard his wife had been awarded custody of their son. He reacted by professing no interest in the fight and was badly beaten. He was to lose touch with his son.

Randolph's two elder brothers were professional boxers, and brother Dick became the first black boxer to win a British title. Mrs Turpin had insisted Dick have first shot. Later when Dick lost the title to Albert Finch, Randolph redeemed the family honor within six months by winning it back with a knockout. He thus became British middleweight champion on 17 October 1950. Four months later he became European champion by knocking out Luc van Dam from Holland in 48 seconds.

On 10 July 1951 an unforgettable fight with Sugar Ray Robinson took place at Earls Court, London. Randy brilliantly outpointed Robinson to become world champion. It was one of the most emotional nights in British boxing, both for a capacity crowd and for those listening to the famous radio commentary.

Turpin was only 23, and, partly through inexperience, lost the return two months later at the New York Polo Grounds. He appeared to have the match well under control when he cut Robinson's eye badly in the ninth, and in the tenth, when Randy ripped it open again, it seemed Robinson might be stopped by the referee. In desperation Robinson threw a long right which Randy took on the chin, going down. When he rose Robinson began pummelling him on the ropes. It was almost the end of the round, and if Randy had had the sense to go down again, the bell would have saved him, and he would probably have stopped Robinson in the next. But he stood taking punishment on the ropes and the referee stepped in with seconds to go. A record crowd for a non-heavyweight contest of 60,437 paid $727,627 to see the fight. While on this trip Randy became very friendly with a girl and this was to lead to much trouble later.

A rubber match with Robinson was not forthcoming, but Randy kept in shape, winning the British light-heavyweight title by stopping Don Cockell in the eleventh. Cockell later went nine with Rocky Marciano.

On 21 October 1953 Turpin was in America again, this time to fight Carl 'Bobo' Olson for the world title vacated by Robinson. Here he immediately ran into the girl of two years earlier, who claimed that he had promised to marry her. Randy had become engaged in the meantime to a Welsh girl and had also recently been cited as co-respondent in a divorce suit. As with Stock years earlier, Turpin was in no mood for the fight with Olson, and was outpointed by a man he should have beaten. After the fight Randy was arrested and charged with assault and rape by his American girlfriend, an affair which was eventually settled out of court.

Turpin came home to marry, but his domestic life was rarely happy afterward. He argued with his brother Dick, whom he had previously respected; others in his family were not friendly toward his new wife. His boxing career continued with many inexplicable ups and downs. He won a Lonsdale belt outright, but was knocked out in 65 seconds in a European bout in Rome by Tiberio Mitri. Finally, a defeat in two rounds by Yolande Pompey in 1962 led him to retire.

Turpin had been careless with his money, spending it on girls, lending it without prospect of return and investing it in businesses which failed. Now the income tax authorities made demands. He used his name wrestling, worked in a scrap metal yard, and finally took a café.

On 17 May 1966, with little money and four daughters to bring up, he went into his bedroom, fired two shots at his youngest child then two at himself, one to the head, the second, fatally, to the heart. For a short time he had been one of boxing's greatest, but whereas he could handle himself in the ring, pressures outside had proved too much for him.

Below left: Turpin receives the world championship trophy.
Below: The British light-heavy win over Don Cockell.
Right: Turpin down in the ninth before losing his 1953 fight with Carl 'Bobo' Olson for the vacant world title.

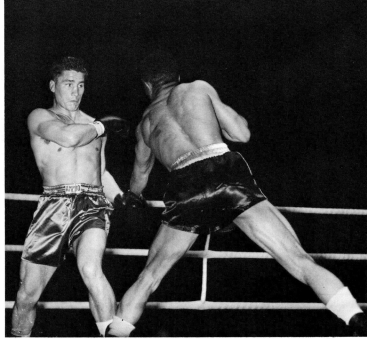

Carlos Monzon
He sought his fortune

When Carlos Monzon first fought outside South America he won the world championship, and many of the world's boxing followers heard of him for the first time. By the time he retired seven years later he had quietly earned recognition as one of the greatest champions in the most competitive of all divisions.

Monzon was born on 7 August 1942 at San Jairer in Santa Fé, Argentina, one of ten children of a poor family. He was not a natural fighter, but took up boxing in a local gymnasium as a healthy occupation for a poor boy. He did well as an amateur and soon realized that professional boxing offered a chance of a better life, as it always has done for boys of impoverished backgrounds. The fact that he set out deliberately to learn the principles of correct boxing later stood him in good stead, when fighting the world's best. He was never at a loss for a move, always remaining cool under pressure and always in command no matter whom he fought.

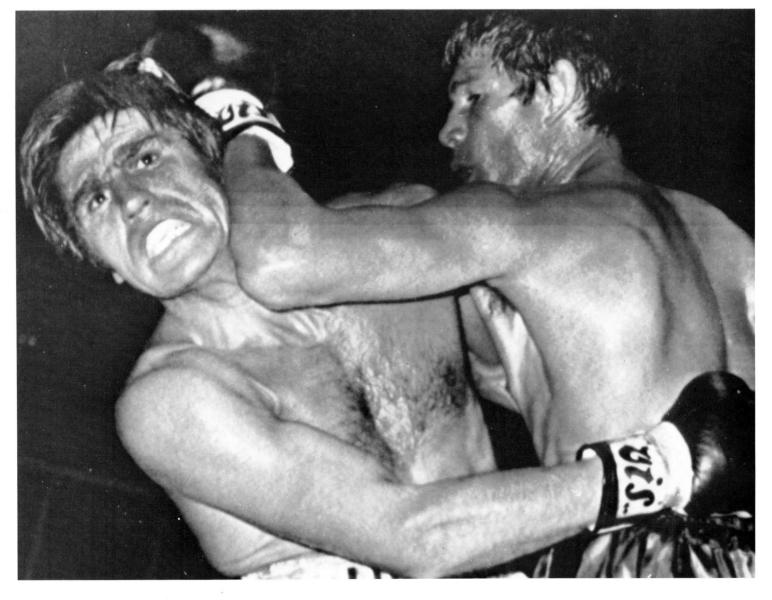

Left: Carlos Monzon, one of the great middleweight champions of recent times, raises his arms in triumph after being presented with his middleweight belt following his defeat of former champion, Emile Griffith, in 1971.

Below left: The stylish champion, Nino Benvenuti of Italy, showing anything but style as he grabs Monzon round the waist in an effort to dodge the blows in their championship fight in Rome. Monzon knocked out Nino in the twelfth round and took the title from him.

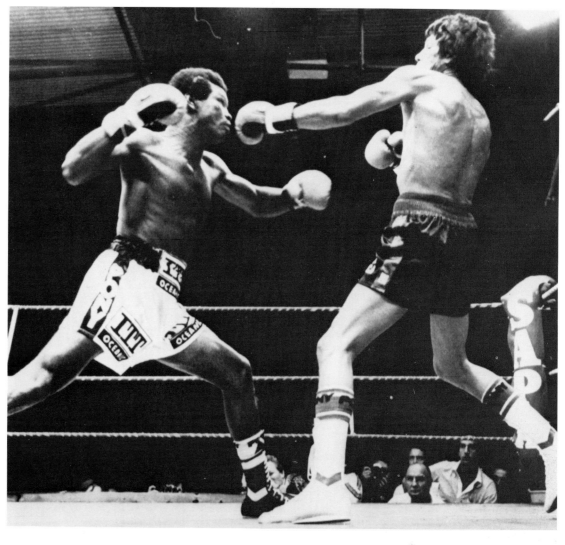

Right: Carlos (right) in his last fight in 1977. He was 35 years old and had reigned unbeaten for seven years. After outpointing challenger Rodrigo Valdes, Carlos decided there was nothing more left to prove in the ring.

Carlos grew into a strong middleweight. In February 1963 he turned professional and in seven years' campaigning in South America had over 80 fights, winning over half inside the distance. Three times early in his career he was beaten on points, the only defeats he was ever to suffer. He outpointed Jorge Fernandez twice, once to win the Argentine title and once the South American.

On 7 November 1970 he took his first long trip, to Rome, to challenge for the undisputed world middleweight title, held by the idol of Italy, Nino Benvenuti, a former Olympic champion and a sophisticated boxer. It was a shock not only for Italians expecting a Roman holiday but for all boxing when Monzon knocked out the great hero Nino with a crushing right to the chin in the twelfth round.

Carlos proved this was no fluke by beating Benvenuti in the third round of a rematch six months later at Monte Carlo, so ending the recent title-holder's career. Another great former champion, Emile Griffith, was then stopped in the fourteenth round in Buenos Aires.

It was clear by now that the 30-year-old Monzon was an outstanding boxer. In 1972 he fought off four challengers: Denny Moyer (USA), stopped in the fifth in Rome, where they now appreciated Monzon's class; Jean-Claude Bouttier (France), the European champion, who retired in the twelfth in Paris; Tom Bogs (Denmark), the next European champion, whom the referee saved in the

fifth in Copenhagen; and Bennie Briscoe (USA), the American champion, outpointed in Buenos Aires.

In 1973 Emile Griffith was again beaten in Monte Carlo (this was a close points decision for the champion) and then Carlos accepted a challenge from the long-reigning welterweight champ, José Napoles (Cuba). The brave but lighter Napoles was forced to retire in the sixth in Paris.

The WBC then withdrew recognition from Monzon for failing to defend against Rodrigo Valdes, who was nominated as their champion. Carlos went on unperturbed, knocking out his opponents to retain the title still recognized by the WBA: Tony Mundine (Australia) went in the seventh in Buenos Aires; Tony Licata (USA) in the tenth in New York; European champion Gratien Tonna (France) in the fifth in Paris.

On 20 June 1976 Monzon took the fight he wanted, a unifying contest with the WBC pretender to his throne, Rodrigo Valdes of Colombia. Carlos was now 34 years old, four years older than Valdes. Nevertheless he outpointed the Colombian comfortably to become once again the undisputed champion. Thirteen months later he repeated the performance in the same ring, and, having seen off all legitimate challengers, retired.

Rome, Paris, Copenhagen, Monte Carlo, New York – it sounds like the itinerary of a jet-set socialite – but this was the route a poor boy from Argentina took to achieve world fame as a middleweight champion.

Marvin Hagler
The Master of Disaster

Marvin Hagler, with his awesome physique, his shaven head, his destructive record, his merciless eyes, his arrogant demeanor and his fierce fighting style was the most impressive and powerful world champion to emerge during the mid-1980s.

The mean way in which Hagler went about his business in the blood and sweat trade was a little deceptive, because outside the ring he was an avowed and gentle family man. Inside the ropes nobody was more professional.

He was born in Newark, New Jersey, on 23 May 1952. An outstanding amateur, he began boxing professionally five days before his 21st birthday in 1973. It took him a long time to establish himself among the contenders and he had to wait until 30 November 1979 before he was given a shot at the undisputed world middleweight title, taking on the Italian Vito Antuofermo in Las Vegas. In the light of Hagler's subsequent career it is astonishing that he could do no better than a draw over 15 rounds, the title staying with Antuofermo.

Marvin had a second chance at the crown on 27 September 1980, when the champion was England's Alan Minter, who had easily beaten Antuofermo on two separate occasions. The fight was held in London and Minter's fans confidently expected him to beat this challenger whose record was relatively unimpressive. Hagler however had made such a mess of Minter's face by the third round that the referee was forced to stop the

Above: Marvelous Marvin Hagler celebrating in the ring with his two championship belts after beating Roberto Duran in 1983.

Left: Hagler won the world title in London in 1980, taking it from Britain's Alan Minter, whose face was to be badly cut by the third round.

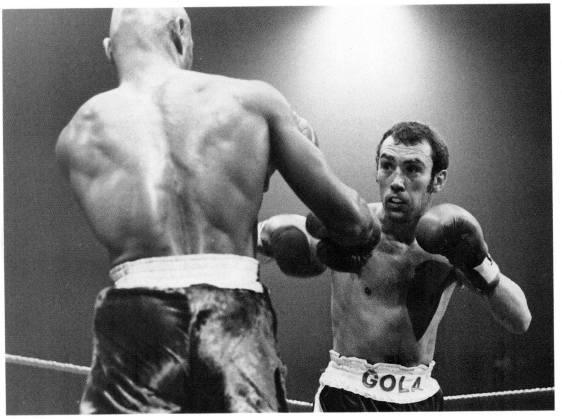

Right above: One of the most exciting fights of all time was the encounter between Hagler and challenger Thomas Hearns at Caesars Palace, Las Vegas, in 1985. It lasted less than three rounds, but was furious action from start to finish.

Right below: John Mugabi gave Hagler stiff opposition in a 1986 challenge, but Marvin eventually inflicted the first defeat on the Ugandan.

contest. Ugly crowd scenes followed as Minter's disappointed followers rained objects into the ring.

Minter retired, and there was no doubt that a very potent fighting force had appeared on the scene. He changed his name to 'Marvelous Marvin Hagler' and proceeded to beat every challenger in his division.

In 1981 Fulgencio Obelmijias of Venezuela, former champion Vito Antuofermo and Mustafa Hamsho of Syria were all halted in a total of 23 rounds. Hagler then speeded up his act, disposing of William 'Caveman' Lee in one round and Obelmijias, in a return in San Remo, Italy, in five.

In February 1983 he took on Minter's successor as British and European champion, Tony Sibson. This fight moved Hagler's standards up another notch, as Sibson was stopped in the sixth round and taken to hospital in a blizzard for 17 stitches in the cuts round his eyes. Welterweight champion Sugar Ray Leonard described Hagler this night as 'awesome'; former champion Minter said he was 'frightening' and a brave Sibson called him a 'master of disaster.'

Wilford Scypion was knocked out in four rounds and Marvelous Marvin's third defense in 1983 was the one that went the distance. It was a battle with the equally marvelous veteran Roberto Duran of Panama, previous holder of the world light and welterweight titles and now in his 17th year of legal professional blood-spilling. In theory Hagler, a natural middleweight, should have dispatched the former lightweight with the thickening waist, but he treated Duran with caution and respect and had to work throughout all 15 rounds for his clear-cut points decision.

Many thought that this fight might have signalled the beginning of Hagler's decline, as he himself was now 31 years old, but he saw off Juan Roldan of Argentina in

Left: The middleweight champion of the 1980s, Marvin Hagler.
Above: Mustafa Hamsho prepares to sit down unwillingly in New York in 1984. He lasted three rounds only.
Right: A jubilant Hagler after his decisive 1985 victory over Hearns, a challenger whom many thought might win.

1984 and Mustafa Hamsho again in a total of 13 rounds, the referee showing mercy to both the losers.

On 15 April 1985 Hagler fought Thomas Hearns (USA), the WBC light-middleweight champion, in a fight which was eagerly awaited and which packed into its eight minutes more action than any of the 15,000 who crowded Caesars Palace, Las Vegas, could remember seeing in any other fight. Hearns, 'The Hit Man,' began, as usual, at great speed, aiming to inflict the maximum damage on the usually slow-starting Hagler in the first round. But Hagler began as never before, and came out of his corner as if he were putting all the ferocity and destruction he had cultivated for years into battering Hearns into instant submission. The result was the most electrifying three minutes of mayhem, each man rocking the other with terrifying blows.

Hagler was cut at the end of that round, but Hearns looked the more bemused. It was too late now for Hearns to change his style and use his long legs to box round Hagler. He had already soaked up enough punishment to make those legs unsteady, and in the second round Hagler's continued relentless onslaught caused Hearns to fight with increasing desperation. Not that he was unsuccessful himself, for twice in the third round the referee asked the ringside doctor to look at the cuts around Hagler's eyes.

After the second of these inspections, Hagler, by now desperate himself, charged across the ring and dealt such a powerful left and right to Hearns that the challenger

spun round and wobbled across the ring looking as if he was walking through water. Hagler followed him and two more solid rights put Hearns down on his back. At nine he climbed up but his legs seemed to have a will of their own, his eyes were glazed and the referee kindly led him to his corner.

Hagler had put on a clever exhibition. A natural strong middleweight, he had banked on being too powerful for Hearns, who was by nature a few pounds lighter, and had put all his strength and skill into a non-stop blitz. It worked.

On 3 March 1986 another worthy challenger, John 'The Beast' Mugabi from Uganda, who had won all 26 of his professional fights by knockouts, kept Hagler engaged for 11 rounds before another 15,000 Las Vegas fans, watching in pouring rain. The hard-hitting Mugabi had the better of it in the early rounds, and it was not until he began to tire with the realization that he was unable to stop the champion that Hagler eventually got on top and knocked his man out midway through the eleventh round.

Marvelous Marvin thus remained the outstanding world champion, supreme in his division. He whetted the appetite of Don Curry, the undisputed welterweight champion, and of Sugar Ray Leonard, the retired welter and light-middleweight champion, who talked of making a $10 million comeback especially to fight him. Certainly any fighter who beats Hagler will have his own claim to greatness, as well as a heavy bag of cash.

Welterweight

The unification bout in 1981 between Thomas Hearns (left), the WBA welterweight champion, and Sugar Ray Leonard, the WBC champion. Leonard won in the fourteenth round.

Ted Kid Lewis
The Crashing Dashing Kid

Ted Kid Lewis will be remembered as the most successful British boxer this century, and, pound for pound, possibly the best. He won a record nine national or international titles. Lewis fought professionally for 20 years, and took part in over 280 contests, no fewer than 42 of which were championship bouts. Thirty of these were world title fights, although about half were of the no-decision kind which were necessary by law in certain parts of America in the days up to 1920.

Lewis was born Gershon Mendelhoff on 24 October 1894 at Aldgate, in London's East End. He joined a local club and developed a liking and great aptitude for boxing. He was not quite 15 years old when he had his first professional contest, and not quite 17 when he won the vacant British and Empire featherweight titles, the referee rescuing Alec Lambert in the seventeenth. This took place in London on 6 October 1913, and four months later the added the European title when Paul Til of France was disqualified in the twelfth round. Shortly afterward Lewis went off to campaign in Australia.

With war looming he went on to America for five years. By now he was a welterweight, but in a busy career he took on both welters and middles. On 21 August 1915 he challenged Jack Britton for the world welterweight championship and won a 12-round decision. He was still only 20 years old. Lewis and Britton held the title between them for over seven years, and met each other 20 times. Lewis beat Britton again and a string of other challengers, but lost the title back to Britton on 20 April 1916 when he was outpointed over 20 rounds at New Orleans. Six times Lewis attempted to regain the title from Britton, but four were no-decision bouts and one a draw – then it was Lewis's turn again with a 20-round points victory at Dayton on 25 June 1917. Lewis defended successfully until 17 March 1919 when Britton knocked him out in the ninth at Canton.

With the war over, Lewis returned to London and claimed the British middleweight title with a fourth-round knockout of Johnny Bee. Next he fought the first of three bouts with another great opponent, Johnny Basham of Newport. Lewis won the British, British

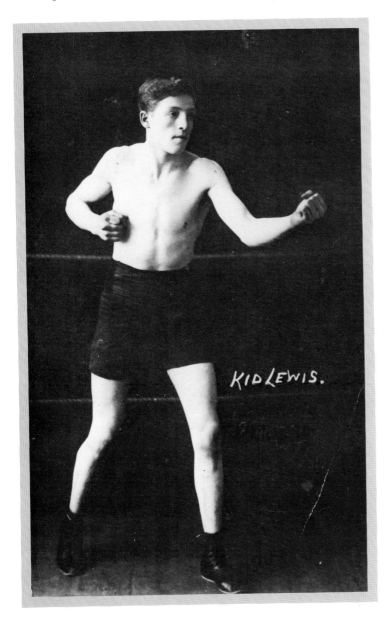

KID LEWIS.

Left: Ted Kid Lewis, one of the most active of all boxers, and one of the best. At the young age of 20 he became world welterweight champion and in 20 years Lewis had nearly 300 fights.

Above right: A decisive victory for the Crashing Dashing Kid. Frankie Burns of Australia is out cold in the eleventh and Lewis wins the vacant British Empire middleweight title in 1922.

Right: Lewis says goodbye to his wife at Waterloo Station, London, having accepted an engagement to fight in South Africa.

Far right: Lewis in training at Shoeburyness in 1923.

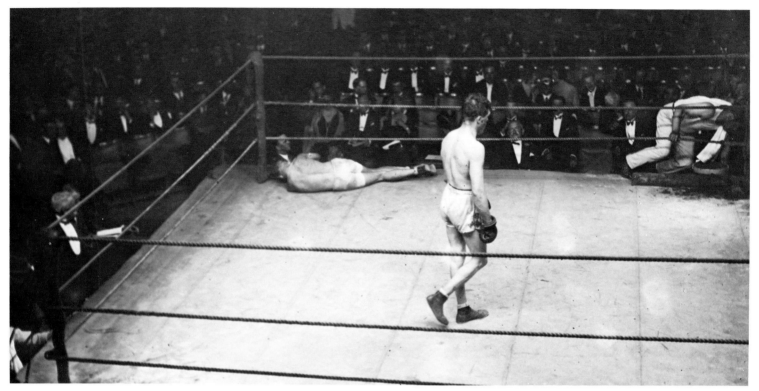

Empire and European welterweight championships with a ninth-round knockout (he was world champion before becoming British champion).

Lewis was an all-action performer who proved a big crowd-pleaser. The 'Crashing Dashing Kid,' as he came to be known, was an aggressive fighter who swarmed all over his opponents.

On 7 February 1921 he returned to New York to try to win back the world welterweight title, but was outpointed over 15 rounds by his old adversary Jack Britton. Back in London later in the year he outpointed Jack Bloomfield over 20 rounds for the undisputed British middleweight title, then took the European title, knocking out Johnny Basham in the twelfth.

The Kid ambitiously stepped up another division in challenging Georges Carpentier on 11 May 1922 for the Frenchman's world light-heavyweight title and European heavyweight title. Unfortunately he had little chance to see if his speed and aggression could take Georges out of his stride, because when the referee spoke to him in the first round he stopped boxing to argue, and Carpentier flashed over a right to his unguarded chin, knocking him out.

Lewis boxed on but gradually lost his titles to up-and-coming challengers. Roland Todd, on his second attempt, took his middleweight titles from him on 15 February 1923, and Tommy Milligan his welterweight titles on 26 November 1924 in Edinburgh. Both defeats were on points over 20 rounds.

The Kid was now past 30 years old. He stayed in the game for another five years before hanging up his gloves. He died in London on 20 October 1970.

Above: Lewis fought Johnny Basham three times in 16 months in 1920 and 1921, with the British, British Empire and European titles at stake. Lewis (right) won all three fights, and something of his style can be gathered from the picture.

Left: Lewis throws a long left at Boy McCormick in London in 1921. McCormick was the British light-heavyweight champion, but Lewis won when the referee stopped the contest in the fourteenth.

Henry Armstrong
Perpetual motion

Henry Armstrong was a phenomenal fighter. He had a very slow heartbeat, which meant that he did not seem to tire as quickly as ordinary people. He was not only capable of 31 pro bouts in one period of 14 months, but he was able to keep up a non-stop attack for three minutes of every round – over half of his opponents failed to last the distance with him.

He was born Henry Jackson on a plantation in Columbus, Mississippi, on 12 December 1912. His paternal grandfather was white, his grandmother a black slave. Armstrong's father married a half-Cherokee Indian, and Armstrong was the eleventh of their 15 children.

Armstrong moved to St Louis as a child where he began boxing as an amateur, although, because he was poor, he frequently accepted money for his 'amateur' appearances. He also had some professional bouts. In 1931, he rode the rails with a friend to San Francisco, and began to fight as an amateur again. Until now, he had been boxing under his real name, Jackson. To lose his old pro record, he took the surname of his trainer, Harry Armstrong. Eventually he became a professional at the end of 1931. He was, however, badly managed, and many of his early professional matches were fought to instructions, often to lose.

After a while Al Jolson, the famous singer, saw him and bought his contract, giving him to Eddie Mead to manage. Mead had once done a favor for Jolson's wife, filmstar Ruby Keeler. Armstrong campaigned successfully as a featherweight, and, after knocking out Mike Belloise, a leading contender, in New York, he obtained a world title match with Petey Sarron on 29 October 1937. Sarron was knocked out in the sixth round. This was the end of a spell in which Armstrong had averaged a contest every two weeks for 14 months.

Armstrong's amazing style and stamina had earned him various epithets, one being 'Hurricane Hank,' but as he continued to knock out all and sundry 'Homicide Hank' became the more popular nickname.

Winning the featherweight title began a purple patch for the 25-year-old Armstrong. On 31 May 1938 he moved up two divisions to welterweight and, giving away over 14 pounds, he outpointed world champion Barney Ross over 15 rounds at New York. The great Ross was given a bad beating and did not fight again. On 17 August 1938 Armstrong went for the in-between title, the lightweight, and by outpointing the tough scrapper Lou Ambers over 15 rounds he became the undisputed world champion at three weights simultaneously, a unique and astonishing record in boxing history.

Henry gave up his featherweight title, being unable to make the weight, and concentrated on the heaviest class of the three, the welterweights. In his first year he defended this title no fewer than seven times, including a trip to London to beat the British champion, Ernie

Above: Henry Armstrong training in 1938.
Below: The work pays off: Armstrong (facing) wins the welterweight title in 1938 after dominating Barney Ross throughout their fight.

Left: Armstrong defended his welterweight title in England and Cuba in 1939, his only defenses outside the USA. Here he shakes hands with Ernie Roderick at the weigh-in for their London contest.

Right: Armstrong stands over Lou Ambers at New York in 1938. He outpointed Lou to take his lightweight crown and create a record of holding three world titles simultaneously.

Below: Armstrong forces Roderick to the ropes in their 1939 title fight at Harringay Arena, London. Roderick gave Armstrong one of his hardest defenses, before losing the points verdict.

Below right: Armstrong receives his world championship trophy. Both he and Roderick show punishment around the eyes.

Roderick. Then on 22 August 1939, having shed weight to return to the lightweights, he defended his title against ex-champion Lou Ambers but this was not a good idea and a weakened Armstrong was outpointed.

He continued to defend his welterweight crown at the same hectic rate as before, until on 1 March 1940 he attempted another record by challenging the world middleweight champion, Ceferino Garcia, whom he had beaten two years earlier as a welterweight. The fight which took place at Los Angeles produced a draw over 10 rounds – Armstrong only just failed to win a world title at a remarkable fourth weight.

The indefatigable Armstrong continued defending his welter title nearly every month, but finally overreached himself when he defended against the very rough Fritzie Zivic only eleven days after his previous defense. This was on 4 October 1940, and Zivic lasted the fierce pace to earn a 15-round points win. Sugar Ray Robinson made his debut on the same bill.

Armstrong was now an ex-champion. He failed to re-gain his title some 15 weeks later when he made a terrific rally before a big crowd at Madison Square Garden, nearly knocking out Zivic after being in trouble and being given one more round by the referee who eventually stopped the fight in the twelfth. Homicide Hank made a comeback 18 months later, and did beat Zivic in a non-title bout, but he lost a later fight to Robinson. Finally he retired early in 1945.

Armstrong had not been allowed to keep too much of what he had earned. After his retirement, he lost money on a West Coast nightspot, Henry Armstrong's Club, and on a film of his life, *Keep Punching*, which summed up his style. He went back to live in St Louis, where he became a director of a boys' club and was ordained in the ministry, becoming assistant pastor at his local church.

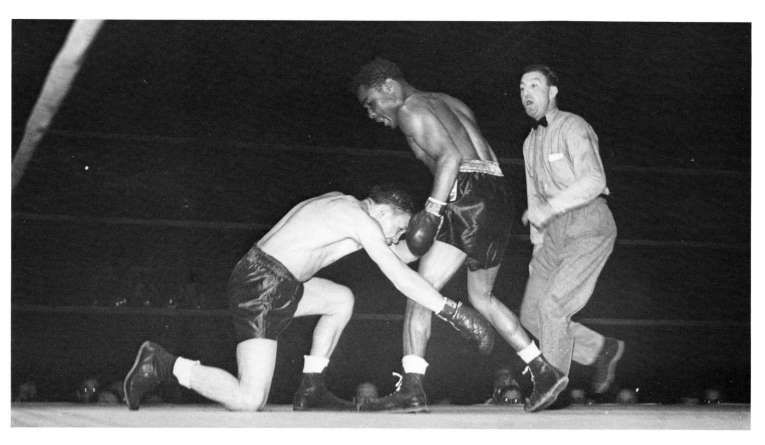

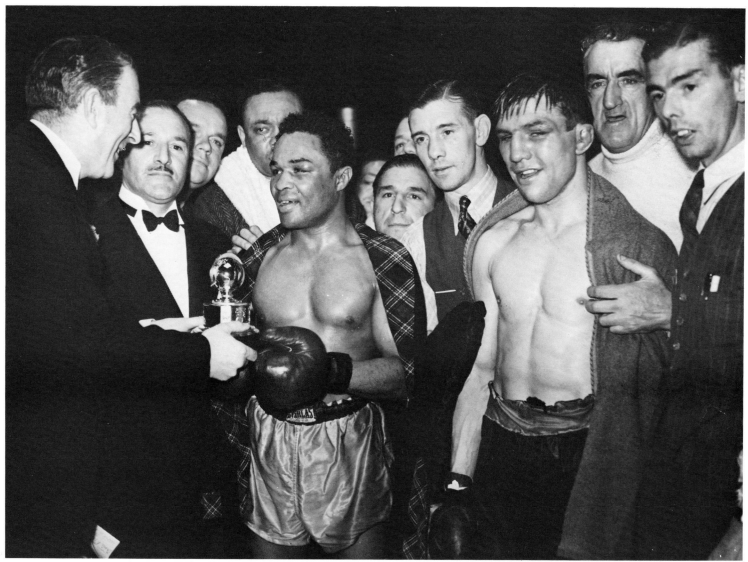

Thomas Hearns
The Hit Man

Few young fighters have caused as much excitement in the blood and guts trade as the up-and-coming Thomas Hearns. Tall, fast, mean, destructive, he appeared to have all the attributes to become one of the greatest boxers of all time. Despite a couple of reverses in title bouts he remains one of the big draws in modern boxing, a man whose motto seems to be 'destroy or be destroyed.'

Hearns was born in Memphis, Tennessee, on 18 October 1958. He grew up on the rough East Side of Detroit, one of nine children. Hearns learned to use his fists and at the age of ten first put on the gloves in the basement of the King Solomon Baptist Church in Detroit. He became an outstanding amateur boxer, and before he was 19 years old he was National Golden Gloves welterweight champion. He immediately turned professional, making his paid debut in November 1977.

None of his first 13 opponents survived the third round. In his 26th fight Angel Espada became the 24th opponent to be stopped and Hearns became the United States Boxing Association welterweight champion. Three fights later, on 2 August 1980, he challenged the WBA world title-holder. Pipino Cuevas of Mexico was himself a knock-out specialist, a man who had been world champion at only 18½ years old, and who had, in

Above: Thomas Hearns, whose 6 foot 2½ inch frame looked to be too skinny to punch hard, rose rapidly to the top by inflicting maximum damage on a number of opponents who could testify to the power of his fists.

Left: Hearns receives inter-round advice from trainer Emanuel Stewart (right). In most of his fights there were not many inter-round intervals.

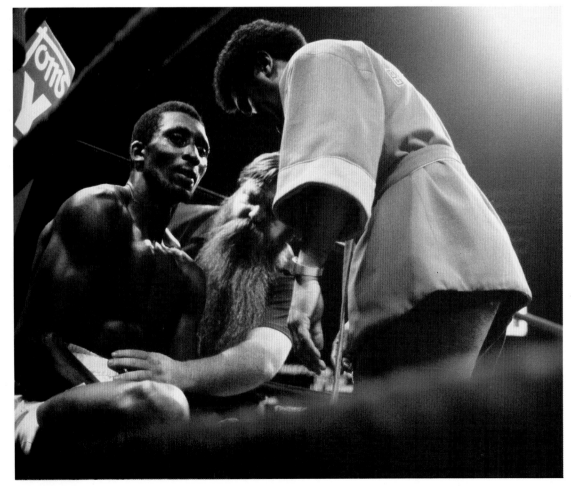

Above right: Hearns forces Sugar Ray Leonard to the ropes in their 1981 unification bout at Caesars Palace, Las Vegas, which drew a record television audience. Hearns faded after a good start and suffered his first defeat.

Right: Most of Hearns's challengers did not test his stamina. Juan Pablo Baez leans helpless on the ropes in the fourth round on 25 June 1981 as the referee leads Hearns away.

his four years' reign, seen off 11 pretenders. Hearns destroyed Cuevas in two rounds, the only knockout defeat in the Mexican's career.

This performance made the hardest-bitten boxing followers sit up. 'Hearns is awesome,' said Muhammad Ali. 'Tommy is just plain mean,' said Dick Mastro, veteran editor of the *Official Boxing Record.* 'Fighters I have fought are never the same as they were,' said Tommy. 'I take good care of my people. I can reach deep inside them and inflict permanent damage.' Hearns, originally called the 'Motor City Cobra' because of his height and reach, earned himself a new nickname, 'The Hit Man,' the name the underworld gives to contract killers. The killer instinct was something the 6 foot 2½ inches, 147 pound Hearns appeared not to be short of.

None of the new champion's first three challengers troubled him unduly: Luis Primera of Venezuela, Randy Shields of the United States, and Juan Pablo Baez of Dominica, all failed to go the distance.

On 16 September 1981 came the dream fight boxing fans had been discussing for a year, a unifying contest between the WBA and WBC welterweight kings: Hearns and Sugar Ray Leonard. It was something of a grudge fight between the two most charismatic men in the fight game. They had known each other as amateurs and when Leonard had turned professional Hearns had worked out with him for five days. There had been some over-enthusiastic sparring which led to some forthright public statements with Hearns expressing a willingness to be the doctor who stitched up Leonard's mouth for him.

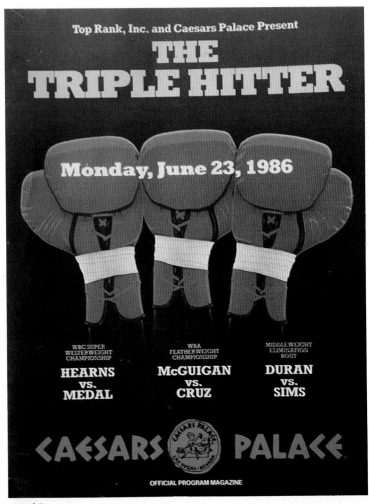

The fight, at Las Vegas, lived up to expectations. At first it went Hearns's way, but just when it looked as if the judges would need to make a tricky decision, Leonard exploded in the fourteenth and the referee was forced to stop the fight in his favor.

Hearns decided to campaign as a light-middleweight and on 3 December 1982 took on Wilfred Benitez of the USA for the WBC world title. Benitez was a worthy opponent, having been the youngest-ever world champion at 16½ when taking the light-welterweight title in 1976. Subsequently he had been welter and light-middleweight champion. Hearns's hitting was enough to win a 15-round points decision at New Orleans, and he was again a world champion. Luigi Minchillo of Italy challenged, and was also outpointed. Then the Hit Man resumed his old ways, leaving the referee to rescue Roberto Duran of Panama and Fred Hutchings of the USA in two and three rounds respectively.

On 15 April 1985 Hearns took on another mighty opponent when challenging Marvin Hagler for his middleweight championship. Many thought Hearns might be the man to upset Hagler, but in three desperate rounds of warfare it was Hearns who wilted.

The Hit Man resumed winning ways when he returned to brood among the light-middleweights and wait for the next million-dollar contract which would enable him to rub out one of his fellow champions.

Left: The poster for a 'triple hitter' at Caesars Palace.
Below: Hearns attacking Mark Medal on the 'triple hitter.' He retained his WBC title in the eighth.

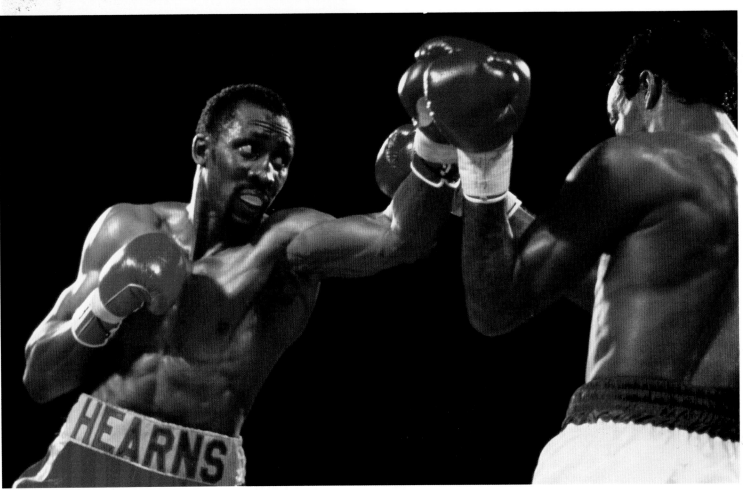

Sugar Ray Leonard
Restless in retirement

When Muhammad Ali's career was on the wane at the end of the 1970s, boxing was losing its greatest-ever character and box-office draw. A new charismatic fighter was needed to fill the void and satisfy the public need for a figurehead. The handsome, flamboyant, dazzling, highly skilled Sugar Ray Leonard, with a Cheshire cat smile, was Ali's natural successor.

Born on 17 May 1956 at Wilmington, South Carolina, Ray Charles (his parents were fans of the singer) Leonard began his career as a brilliant amateur boxer. He was a Golden Gloves lightweight champion in 1973 and light-welterweight champion in 1974. In 1976 in Montreal he was the Olympic light-welterweight gold medalist, boxing with a photograph of his girlfriend and two-year-old son on his shoes.

Sugar Ray (since Sugar Ray Robinson, all good boxing Rays are likely to have 'Sugar' added) made his professional debut on 5 February 1977, winning a six-round points decision over Luis Vega of the USA. It proved all wins for him as he took the American welterweight title in 1979 by stopping Pete Ranzany in four rounds.

On 30 November 1979 he challenged Wilfred Benitez for the WBC welterweight title. Benitez himself was an outstanding boxer, having become in 1976 the youngest ever to win a world title. The pair put up a terrific show, with Leonard finally getting the upper hand, forcing the referee to stop the fight only six seconds before the end of the fifteenth round. This really established Leonard as a boxer of the highest rank, a position confirmed when he outclassed Dave 'Boy' Green of Britain, by knocking him out in the fourth at Landover. On 20 June 1980 Leonard suffered his only defeat when he returned to Montreal, the city of his Olympic triumph, to defend his title against Roberto Duran of Panama. He was unanimously outpointed in this fight by the rough, tough, hustling challenger. It is a measure of Leonard's drawing power that he was able to collect $8½ million for this fight.

Above: Sugar Ray Leonard, one of the greatest of modern champions, whose career was cut short by an eye injury but whose love affair with the ring caused continual thoughts of a comeback.

Left: Leonard, facing camera, one of the most impressive Olympic champions of 1976, cashed in by turning professional early in 1977.

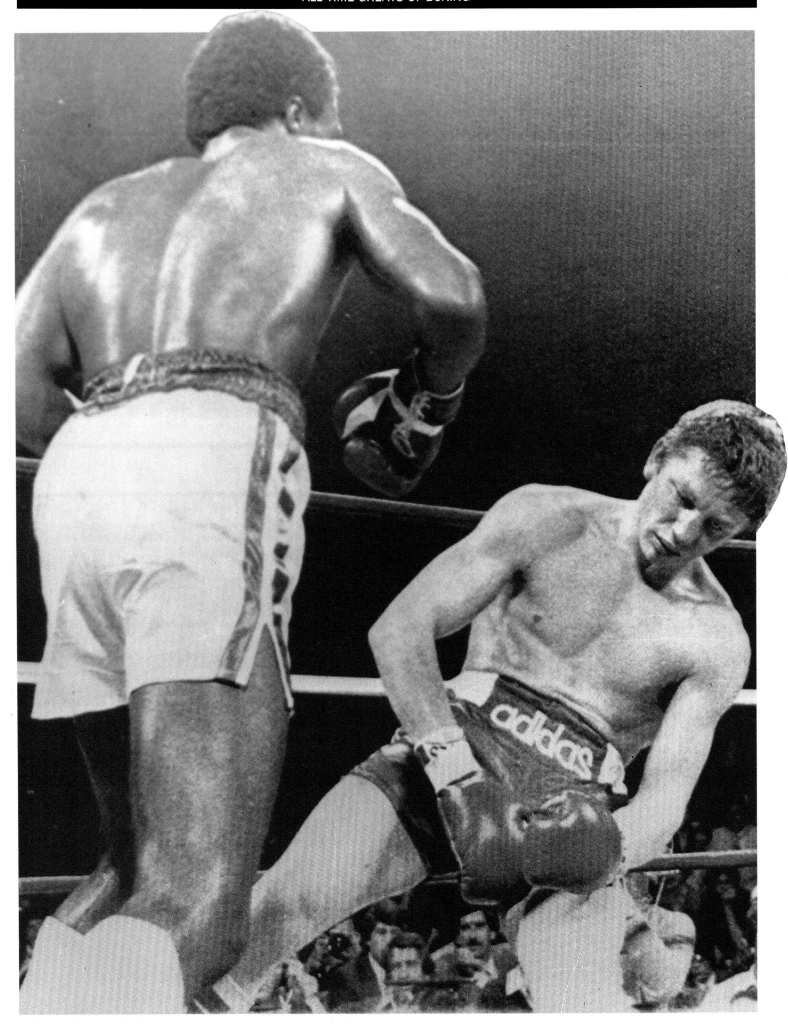

Left: Dave 'Boy' Green sinks in the fourth at Landover.
Above: Leonard and Hearns in their celebrated 1981 battle.
Right: A new experience for Leonard as he lies flat on his back in his comeback fight with Kevin Howard in May 1984.

If this result was surprising, the return was sensational. On 28 November an inspired Leonard so outboxed and tantalized Duran that the demoralized macho man, who had never before even taken a backward step, remained sitting on his stool when the bell rang for the ninth round.

Sugar Ray disposed of Larry Bonds in the tenth at Syracuse in 1981, then on 25 June went after a second world title. He knocked out Ayub Kalule of Uganda in the ninth at Houston to collect the WBA light-middleweight championship. However he soon gave this up to concentrate on the welter division. A unifying title fight between Leonard and the WBA champion, the exciting newcomer Thomas Hearns, was an attraction that promised to break all records. It did, for when the two met in Las Vegas on 16 September 1981 Leonard was paid $11 million, the biggest purse in history.

Nor did the fans begrudge a cent of it, for the fight was one of the best of all time. Hearns began in his usual explosive manner, and more than once seemed on the point of victory as his blows shook Sugar Ray. But Leonard had proven stamina whereas Hearns had a tendency to fade, and in the fourteenth a sustained comeback assault by Leonard forced the referee to intervene and Leonard became the undisputed champion.

Tragedy set in for Sugar Ray, however. After easily beating Bruce French in February 1982, he was forced to undergo an eye operation for a detached retina, and on 9 November 1982 he announced his retirement.

Sugar Ray's decision did not last. Although he was always careful of his good looks, and was an intelligent man who knew the risks of boxing, particularly after eye trouble, he was also a natural fighter. In May 1984 he made a comeback, knocking out Kevin Howard of the USA in the ninth round. But he was not impressive, and was put down for the first time in his career. Disappointed, he immediately retired again, saying 'I wasn't there. I was apprehensive of being hit.'

In 1986, when he was 30 years old, the lure of the ring tugged again. He announced he wanted to fight the great middleweight, Marvin Hagler. Leonard claimed that after fighting Hearns, Duran and Benitez, it was difficult to get excited by a contest with Kevin Howard, but he badly wanted to beat Hagler. He was a rich man, with a wife and son and a lovely house in Potomac, Maryland. His career earnings of around $30 million brought in a reputed $3,000 a day, a man with everything and nothing to prove. He could be content, but he did not want contentment. He wanted to fight Hagler. He was a true fighting man.

Don Curry
Will the cobra strike?

In 1983, Don Curry, nicknamed the Cobra, followed Wilfred Benitez, Roberto Duran, Thomas Hearns and Sugar Ray Leonard as the world welterweight champion – an illustrious line of succession. There were those who said that Curry would prove the best of the lot, that he was the best pound-for-pound fighter in the world.

Born in Fort Worth, Texas, on 31 December 1961, Curry became a boxer early in his schooldays and claimed to have fought some 400 amateur contests. He was the Golden Gloves welterweight champion in 1980, and the American boycott of the Moscow Olympic Games deprived him of an almost certain gold medal. After turning professional, he quickly became American welterweight champion, recognized in 1982 by both the North American Boxing Federation and the United States Boxing Association.

With Sugar Ray Leonard's retirement as world champion in 1982, Curry found himself, after only 15 professional fights, boxing Jun-Sok Hwang of South Korea for the WBA version of the vacant title. The fight took place on 13 February 1983 at Fort Worth. It was a hard one for Curry, who was knocked down by the Korean and suffered injury to his right hand after punching his opponent in the head. At the end of the 15 rounds Curry was given the verdict and the title after a very punishing bout.

Six months later, in his first defense, he knocked out Roger Stafford in the first round in Sicily. His next fight was a very different affair, another tough one against the highly rated Marlon Starling. Starling managed to take Curry the full distance, although the Cobra was a convincing points winner in the end.

Curry was noticeably protective of his hands, and did not use the normal heavy punchbag in training, but confined himself to a light inflatable version, dismissed by detractors as a balloon. However, no hand weaknesses were apparent to his next two 1984 opponents, Elio Diaz of Venezuela who was forced to retire in the seventh at Fort Worth, and Nino La Rocca who was knocked out in the sixth at Monte Carlo.

Although not as lanky as Hearns who is exceptionally tall for his weight, Curry is tall for a welter at 5 feet 10½ inches and has long arms. He is a brilliant defensive fighter, holding his arms well up and presenting a difficult target. He watches his opponents with intense concentration, stalking them, moving in close and shooting out his long arms to land his blows with force. He has a sharp eye for an opening, very fast hands, and times his punches to perfection. He is also no slouch at the inside brawling, using his elbows and shoulders. It is not long before his opponents begin to feel the effect of his non-stop hustling.

Certainly Colin Jones of Britain, his next opponent, felt his power early in their match on 19 January 1985 at Birmingham. Jones had already fought a draw and lost a narrow points decision to the WBC champion, Milton McCrory of the USA, before meeting Curry in the ring. Early on in the fight Curry opened a gash on the bridge of Jones's nose, obliging the referee to intervene in the fourth round.

The next match was a title unifying contest with Milton McCrory at Las Vegas on 6 December 1985. The sharp and merciless Curry destroyed McCrory, knocking him out in the second to become the undisputed world champion.

Curry was equally impressive on his 1986 reappearance at Fort Worth when he again knocked out his opponent in the second, this time Eduardo Rodriguez of Panama. After this there was a hiatus in Curry's career. For some time Curry had had difficulty in making the welter limit of 147 pounds, and a program taking in Mike McCallum, the WBA light-middleweight king, and eventually middleweight Marvin Hagler was expected. But a June 1986 meeting with McCallum was mysteriously cancelled. It transpired that Curry and his manager Dave Gorman had not been seeing eye to eye, and that Curry was anxious about how his hands would cope with hitting the bigger boys.

Boxing fans wondered if Curry was the new Sugar Ray Leonard after all, or whether he, too, would be halted in mid-career. Later in 1986 he fought the unfancied British and European champion Lloyd Honeyghan. Honeyghan astonished the Atlantic City fans by taking an early lead and then stopping Curry with a badly cut eye at the end of the sixth round. The boxing world wondered – would the 1986 mood of introspection and uncertainty call the tune and so end Curry's career, or would the Cobra strike again?

Above left: Curry went to Monaco to defend his WBA title against Nino La Rocca in 1984. La Rocca succumbed in the sixth, and there was no need for Curry's handlers to change the message on their backs. There was later, when the Cobra became undisputed champion.

Above: Curry lands a left to Colin Jones's face in their title contest at Birmingham. Curry proved too hot for Jones, splitting his nose and causing the referee to stop the fight.

Right: In the same fight Curry holds his arms well up and presents a difficult target for Colin Jones, who fights back off the ropes.

Alexis Arguello of Nicaragua (left) misses with a right to the head of Rey Tam of the Philippines in Los Angeles in 1978, and takes a right to the shoulder. Arguello retained his WBA junior lightweight title when the referee stepped in in the fifth round.

Lightweight

Roberto Duran
One strange lapse

Roberto Duran was the epitome of the public's image of a boxer. Rough, tough, from a poor part of a poor country, he seemed to set out to make 'machismo' a way of life. He would enter the ring unshaven and, eschewing the 'noble art of self-defence,' would batter his opponents with a style resembling street fighting. He never took a backward step – except once. Then he set about rehabilitating his macho image with the biggest test of all.

Duran was born in Guarare, Panama, on 16 June 1951. He showed a great aptitude for fighting, making his professional debut before his 16th birthday. Duran started his career by losing four early contests, but then began an unbeaten run of over 50 fights which saw him dominate the world's lightweights for eight years and then win two more world crowns when he took on the champions at three higher weights.

Duran's long list of world title fights began on 26 June 1972 when he challenged Ken Buchanan of Scotland, the classy WBA lightweight champion, at Madison Square Garden, New York. As the bell rang to end the thirteenth round Buchanan sank to the canvas, clutching his groin and claiming a late foul blow. He was unable to continue, and the referee awarded the fight and title to Duran despite his rough-house tactics.

Roberto settled into a two-fight-a-year routine, seeing off the world's best. His first four defenses were in Panama City, where he built up a fanatical following. Jimmy Robertson of the USA was knocked out in five, Hector Thompson of Australia stopped in eight, Ishumatsu Susuki of Japan in ten, and Esteban de Jesus of Puerto Rico, who held a decision over Duran, was knocked out in eleven. Duran then travelled a short distance to San Juan, Costa Rica, to dispose of Mastaka Takayama of Japan in the first, returned to Panama City to knock out Ray Lampkin of the USA in the fourteenth, and then left his knockout even later in San Juan, Puerto Rico, when Mexican Leoncio Ortiz went down in the fifteenth and last round.

Duran defended in the United States after that, but the results were the same, Lou Bizzaro of the USA, Alvaro Rojas of Costa Rica and Vilomar Fernandez of Dominica being knocked out in 14, 1 and 13 rounds respectively. Then Edwin Viruet of Puerto Rico earned a little niche among lightweights by taking Duran the distance. Meanwhile Roberto's old adversary, Esteban de Jesus, had become WBC champion. Duran established his outright lightweight superiority by knocking out his old opponent in the twelfth at Las Vegas. This was 21 January 1978, but having unified the division, Duran relinquished the title undefeated in 1979 to move up to the welters.

Nobody gave Duran much of a chance when on 20 June 1980 he faced the brilliant Sugar Ray Leonard in Montreal for the latter's welterweight title. It was a classic encounter, however, with Leonard boxing well but Duran hustling at close quarters, and the amazing Roberto took the points verdict and a new title.

On 28 November 1980 there was an inexplicable lapse in Duran's fighting. In a return with Leonard at New Orleans, the macho man was dazzled by his opponent's brilliant boxing. From the start Leonard taunted him, landing punches and taking few in return, and in the eighth Duran, still apparently fit and strong, turned his back and gave up. His multitude of fans in Panama were astounded by this waving of a white flag.

Duran moved up to the light-middleweights to restore his prestige, but in 1982 was outpointed by Wilfred Benitez in Las Vegas when he attempted to take the WBC title. However, he looked to the WBA champion, and on 16 June 1983 took his third world title when in New York the referee stopped Davey Moore's defense in the eighth round.

This victory came on Duran's 32nd birthday, but the veteran still needed a supreme challenge to redeem his reputation, and on 10 November 1983 he challenged Marvin Hagler, the fearsome long-reigning king of the middleweights. Although Hagler was less than a year younger than Duran and Duran had built up his weight for the contest, most thought Duran had bitten off more then he could chew. However, at Caesars Palace, Las Vegas, the typically unshaven and snarling Duran put up one of his bravest scrambling, scrapping performances, and Hagler, for the first time in eight defenses, was taken the distance.

Duran had a shot at the WBC light-middleweight title on 16 June 1984 at Las Vegas, but Thomas Hearns stopped him in the second round. It seemed that this would be his last world title contest. He had faced the very best boxers from light to middleweight and had held three world championships over a period of more than 10 years. A defeat on a split decision by Robbie Sims, Hagler's brother, in June 1986 seemed to presage a fighting end to a great career in which only once did he refuse to mix it.

Left: Roberto Duran, whose forté was rugged, non-stop aggression, with little regard or need for niceties.

Right: The typical Duran. He has champion Ken Buchanan on the ropes in the eleventh round at Madison Square Garden on 26 June 1972, and the referee rushes to sort out both boxers.

Below: Duran was still punching 16 years after taking Buchanan's title. He lost a split decision to Robbie Sims (left) at Las Vegas in June 1986.

Alexis Arguello
Have title, will travel

Alexis Arguello was not a flamboyant fighter. Tall and slim, he was an excellent boxer, who preferred to weigh up his opponents and spot their weaknesses before clinically and efficiently destroying them. That he possessed punching power to back up his boxing ability is shown by the fact that over three-quarters of his victims failed to last the distance. He was one of the best boxer-fighters to come from the champion breeding grounds of Central and South America.

Arguello was born on 19 April 1952 in Managua, the capital of Nicaragua. He showed such skill with his fists that he turned to professional boxing for a career, taking his first contest in his home town when only 16½ years old. In his first five years he suffered two defeats while winning 35 bouts, most of them inside the distance, a convincing record which earned him a shot at the WBA featherweight title, held by Ernesto Marcel of Panama. The contest took place in Panama City on 16 February 1974 and Arguello was outpointed.

However Marcel retired, and before the end of the year Arguello was matched with the new champion, Ruben Olivares, whom he knocked out in the thirteenth round. At the age of 22 Arguello had become champion. As Olivares was soon to become WBC champion, Arguello could justly claim to be the world's top featherweight. In 1975 he successfully defended three times: Leonel Hernandez of Venezuela lasted eight rounds, Rigoberto Riasco of Panama two, and Royal Kobayaski of Japan, whom Arguello fought in Tokyo, five. The last two were later to become light-featherweight world champions.

After knocking out Mexican Salvador Torres in the third round in Inglewood on 19 June 1976, Arguello relinquished the title at the end of the year to campaign in the junior lightweight class. On 28 January 1978 he was given a shot at the WBC world title. Champion Alfredo Escalera of Puerto Rico had already fought off ten challengers but the referee was forced to intervene in the thirteenth round in San Juan. In a superlative display Arguello won his second world title.

For over two years, Alexis was busy and successful seeing off eight opponents. He fought in New York, Los Angeles, Las Vegas, Puerto Rico and Rimini, Italy. Only Arturo Leon of Mexico took him the 15 rounds. Among his other victims were four former or future world champions: Escalera again, Rafael Limon of Mexico, Bobby Chacon of the USA and Rolando Navarrete of the Philippines.

In 1980, Alexis found it necessary to relinquish his second world title, and move up a division to lightweight. On 21 June 1981 he challenged the WBC champion, Jim Watt of Scotland. Watt, who was a month short of his 33rd birthday, was enjoying a late flourish to his career, having made four successful defenses since winning the title, three against Americans. All these were in his native Glasgow, where he enjoyed fanatical support, but

he fought Arguello in London and, although putting up his usual clever display, he was outpointed.

Alexis then embarked on his third career as a world champion, and in the next year disposed of four challengers from the USA, including Ray Mancini, who was to become champion the following year, and James Buscene, four times Golden Gloves champion. All of these fights took place in American rings and none of them went the distance.

In 1982 Arguello attempted to set a record by taking a world title at a fourth weight. On 22 November he challenged Aaron Pryor of Cincinnati for the WBA light-welterweight championship. Pryor was at his peak. Champion for just over two years, he was unbeaten, only two of his fights having gone the distance. He was regarded as something of a wild man, both inside and outside the ring, a complete contrast to the smooth, gentlemanly Arguello. But Arguello's long winning record made him the 11-5 favorite when they met at the Orange Bowl, Miami.

For once the body attacks and clean punching of Alexis could not halt the younger and stronger man. After one of the great exhibitions of all-action boxing and slugging the referee intervened in the fourteenth round as Pryor pummelled a slumped Arguello on the ropes. While Pryor stood holding his hands high in triumph, Alexis slid down the ropes to the canvas and lost consciousness for several minutes. He had shown outstanding courage in the face of defeat.

Nearly a year later he challenged Pryor again, but was knocked out in the tenth round. He relinquished his lightweight crown – the third world title he had given up undefeated. Each of these he had won in his opponent's territory, and during his eight years as a champion he had fought the best in four weights, nearly always in foreign rings. He was an outstanding champion.

Below: Diego Alcala of Panama looks dazed in the first round as he challenges for the WBC junior lightweight title in 1978.
Right: Delight among his supporters as Alexis takes the WBC lightweight crown from Jim Watt.

Featherweight

Sandy Saddler (left) and Willie Pep in their second fight. Pep won this one to ensure a third meeting.

Sandy Saddler
A long feud with Pep

Sandy Saddler stood 5 feet 8½ inches tall and had a reach of 70 inches, as much as some heavyweights. But as Saddler was only a featherweight, he naturally stood out in his division as somewhat freakish. As he was also an extremely hard puncher, it is not surprising that 103 of his 144 wins were by the knockout route.

Sandy (real name Joe) Saddler was born in Boston, Massachusetts, on 23 June 1926, but was brought up in Harlem. He liked boxing and would train after school. He lost three or four of 50 amateur bouts and, finding that opponents steered clear of him, turned professional in 1944, three months before his 18th birthday. He was stopped by Jock Leslie in his second fight, for the only time in his career. In his second year he won 14 consecutive fights by knockouts, seven of which took place in the first round.

It took Saddler 94 fights and over four years to earn a world title fight with one of the great featherweight champions, Willie Pep, the clever 'Will o' the Wisp.' Even then Pep's guaranteed purse left little for Sandy. However he caused one of the surprises of the year by putting Pep down for the first time in a long career and then knocking him out in the fourth.

That was on 29 October 1948, and fifteen weeks later nearly 20,000 fans returned to Madison Square Garden to see if he could do it again. This time Pep put up one of the great exhibitions of boxing, dazzling Saddler with his speed, footwork and clever defensive skills to win a clear-cut points victory over 15 rounds.

Willie Pep kept Saddler waiting 18 months for the obvious rubber match, defending his title three times, while Sandy went on tour and won over 20 contests. The third title fight between Pep and Saddler drew nearly 40,000 fans to Yankee Stadium to see what has always been a classic crowd-pleaser: the brilliant boxer against the destructive puncher.

Pep boxed brilliantly again but Saddler caught him in the third, putting him down. This time, however, Pep recovered to continue his defensive, points-stealing artistry, and Saddler had to work hard to get his heavy blows home. Surprisingly Pep did not come out for the eighth round, claiming an injured shoulder, and Saddler was champion again.

Pep's corner clamored for another return, but Saddler kept him waiting a year. There was little love lost between the two men. Saddler thought he had been discriminated against racially in his long haul to the title and was not happy with a reputation he had for being a 'dirty' fighter. He claimed he was held so much by opponents that frequently he had to wrestle to get free. The three Pep versus Saddler battles so far had been ruthless affairs, but the fourth was the worst.

At the Polo Grounds on 26 September 1951, the two

Left and below: Saddler training (left) and after beating Pep at Madison Square Garden in October 1948 (below).
Right: Pep goes down in the title fight in 1948, knocked out for the first time in 136 bouts. Saddler's victory was one of the surprises of the year.

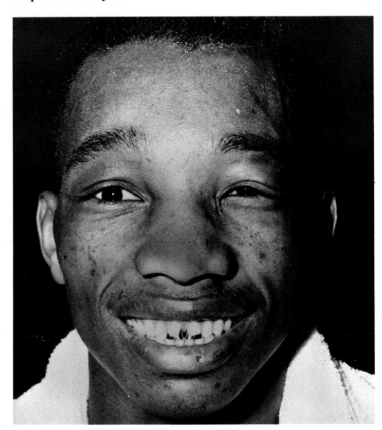

men fouled each other constantly. Saddler opened a deep cut under Pep's eye in the second, allegedly with his thumb, and floored him. In the sixth and eighth they wrestled each other to the floor. Saddler's manager was arguing with a judge when Pep's corner decided he could not come out for the tenth round. Saddler thus won the series three to one, but both boxers were suspended from further fights for six months by the New York State boxing commissioners.

Saddler was, in any case, called up for two years' army service and did not resume his career until 1954, when he knocked out contender Ray Famechon in Paris. Then on 25 February 1955, he outpointed the interim champion, Teddy 'Red Top' Davis, over 15 rounds in New York. He made one defense in 1956, stopping Flash Elorde in the thirteenth. Soon afterwards his eye was injured when a taxi in which he was travelling was involved in a collision, and he was forced to retire. He became a physical training director in a naval gymnasium where he trained professional boxers, being in George Foreman's corner when he fought Ali. In later years Saddler claimed to have become friends with Pep, but he never became reconciled to the fact that Pep's reputation appeared to be greater than his own.

Barry McGuigan
The desert was too hot

The title of Barry McGuigan's biography is *Leave the Fighting to McGuigan*. It is a reference to the sectarian warfare in Ireland. Barry is from the Republic of Ireland, just south of the border with Northern Ireland. He represented Northern Ireland in the 1978 Commonwealth Games and the Republic of Ireland in the 1980 Olympic Games. He is a Catholic and he is married to a Protestant. Their marriage took place in a Protestant church and they went off immediately to a ceremony in a Catholic church. Nobody is more anti-sectarian than Barry. By the time he reached world challenger status he had all Ireland and Britain, irrespective of religion, supporting him.

He was born Finbar McGuigan in Clones, County Monaghan, Republic of Ireland, on 28 February 1961. He began boxing at the age of 12, and after a promising amateur career he turned professional in 1981. Of his first 14 contests in 1981 and 1982, only three went the distance, and one of these he lost to Peter Eubanks, one of boxing twins. It was Barry's third bout, and he avenged the defeat four months later. In 1983 he stopped Vernon Penprase in the second round for the vacant British featherweight title, and went on to knock out Valerio Nati of Italy in six for the vacant European crown.

Barry was proving to be an all-action fighter with unlimited stamina who kept coming forward. He had strong shoulders and a knockout punch in both fists. He was a particularly strong body puncher and stopped many opponents with repeated left hooks to the rib cage.

In 1984 he fought a tough match with Charm Chiteule of Zambia in a Commonwealth title final eliminator. Next he took on his hardest opponent to date, José Caba of the USA, who had just gone the distance with the world champion Eusebio Pedroza. Caba took a beating in a brilliant display by McGuigan which forced the referee to stop the fight in the seventh. This was one of a series of bouts in the King's Hall, Belfast, where Barry had built up a following of roof-raising proportions.

His defense of the European title against Esteban Eguia of Spain, in London, brought an innovation. McGuigan, who had kept the Protestants on his side by refusing to associate himself with the flag of the Republic of Ireland, was now asked to enter the ring under the Union Jack, Britain's flag and symbolic of Northern Ireland's British connection. So as not to offend Catholics, McGuigan demurred, and instead adopted the flag of peace as his standard.

Eguia was knocked out in the third, and Juan LaPorte of Puerto Rico, recent world champion, was next in line to test McGuigan. An emphatic points victory paved the way for the world title shot on 8 June 1985. To Barry's disappointment the match was held in London, not Belfast. Nevertheless, it seemed half Ireland was there. Eusebio Pedroza, of Panama, was a great champion who had reigned for seven years and was making his twentieth defense. The fight was an exciting one, with all the wiles of the champion and his corner unable to

Above right: Barry McGuigan tries a left to the face of Eusebio Pedroza in the WBA featherweight title fight at the Queen's Park Rangers soccer ground, Loftus Road, London in 1985. McGuigan took the title from the veteran champion.

Right: A happy new champion, submerged among fans and journalists.

Left: McGuigan and Danilo Cabrera attempt simultaneous lefts at Dublin in 1986. Barry retained his title, but found Las Vegas a less amenable environment four months later.

withstand the youth, strength and ambition of the challenger. Down in the seventh, staggering in the ninth, nearly stopped in the thirteenth, Pedroza saw his crown pass at last to McGuigan on a unanimous decision.

McGuigan, handsome, modest and articulate, became a hero whose influence spread far wider than the fight game. The 'Clones Cyclone,' as he was called, dissolved a little of the religious hatred which has poisoned life in Ireland for so long.

Three months after his title victory he returned to the King's Hall to force Bernie Taylor to retire in the seventh. In 1986 Danilo Cabrera of the Dominican Republic was stopped in the fourteenth in Dublin.

Barry then set off to woo America and make his fortune on American television. On 23 June 1986 he defended at Caesars Palace, Las Vegas, against a Texan plumber, Steve Cruz. Cruz was a substitute, ranked ninth among the WBA contenders. He was not expected to be a threat. But Cruz was at home in the conditions of the night. The paler McGuigan found the 110 deg F (43 deg C) heat oppressive. He had no strength, and could not nail Cruz who boxed more economically, and from the tenth onward Barry was practically exhausted. In the last round he was dropped twice, enough to guarantee the verdict for Cruz.

In one hour of desert heat, the hero had bitten the dust.

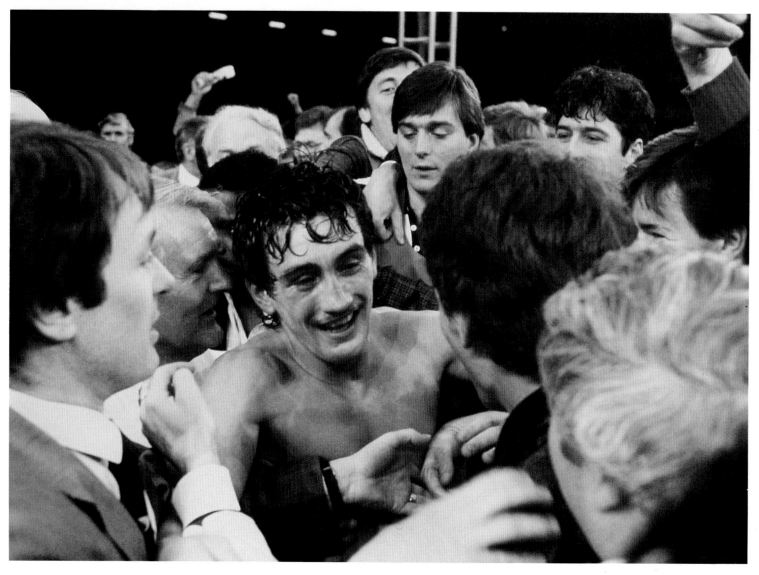

Bantamweight

Ruben Olivares
Pocket knockout king

Many great punchers in the lighter weights have come from Mexico. Among the hardest hitters and greatest champions of all was the square-shouldered bantamweight Ruben Olivares, a pocket Hercules who knocked out over three-quarters of his opponents in a long career.

Olivares was born in Mexico City on 14 January 1947. He was not of the usual poor family, and ate well enough to build up his muscles. He enjoyed boxing and had soon beaten all the local amateurs. When he was 17 he married, and decided to try to make a living fighting for money. His knockout punch was so remarkable that in less than six years, during which time Olivares remained unbeaten, he had managed to notch up 50 victories, 49 of them inside the distance.

Lionel Rose, the tough Australian Aborigine world champion, was brought to Inglewood, California, on 22 August 1969 to face Olivares, and Ruben set to work in his usual manner, displaying a terrific left hook and completely overpowering Rose, who was knocked out in the fifth round.

The new champion's first defense came less than four months later, when Britain's Alan Rudkin was defeated, also at Inglewood. Rudkin was a classy boxer who had already gone the distance in close fights with the previous champions, Fighting Harada and Lionel Rose, but he could stay for only two rounds on his third attempt at the title.

Olivares, the pocket Marciano, was a big draw around Los Angeles with his exciting style. Another money-spinner took place in April 1970 in a battle with fellow-Mexican Jesus Chucho Castillo. Ruben won only on points this time, and took a count. But his purse of $100,000 represented a big payday for a bantam. He was in for a shock, however, when he met Castillo for a return in October. He fought with an injured eye from the first round, and although putting up enormous resistance was stopped by the troublesome eye in the fourteenth. It was his first defeat.

He regained the title in April 1971 by outpointing Castillo, and six months later defended in Japan when the referee stopped the attempt of Kazuyoshi Kanazawa in the fourteenth round. Before the year was out another countryman, Jesus Pimentel, was stopped in the eleventh in Inglewood. Olivares was then knocked out for the first time. Yet another Mexican, Rafael Herrera, did the trick in the eighth at Mexico City.

Olivares then forsook the bantams, where he was having difficulty making the weight, to take on the featherweights. When Ernesto Marcel retired in 1974 Olivares was named by the WBA to meet Zensuke Utagawa for the vacant title. At Inglewood on 9 July 1974 Ruben stopped the Japanese boxer in the seventh to win his second world title. Four months later, however, Ruben suffered his second knockout and lost his crown when Alexis Arguello of Nicaragua stopped him in the thirteenth round.

He was still not done with world titles, for on 20 June 1975 he took on the WBC champion, Bobby Chacon. Chacon was so badly hurt that the referee came to his assistance and stopped the fight in the second. Keeping up his busy schedule, Ruben defended his new title exactly three months later, but again lost on his first defense when he was outpointed by the British Commonwealth champion, David Kotey of Ghana.

Olivares kept campaigning, and nearly four years later, in July 1979, earned another tilt at the WBA title which was firmly held by the outstanding Eusebio Pedroza of Panama. Ruben, by now a 32-year-old veteran, was stopped in the twelfth round. He had four more contests over the next two years, and then decided to retire in 1981 and indulge his liking for expensive cars.

Left: Ruben Olivares digs a hard right into the heavy punchbag in training for his 1969 world bantamweight title fight with Lionel Rose.

Right: The British Empire champion, Alan Rudkin, was knocked out in the second round when he was the first to challenge the new champion, Olivares, in 1969.

Flyweight

Pascual Perez (right) jolts
Oscar Suarez during their
world championship fight at
Montevideo in July 1956.

Jimmy Wilde
The Mighty Atom

When Jimmy Wilde first arrived to box at the famous Blackfriars Ring, the promoter's wife mistook him for a child. Wilde had to insist he was married and well able to take care of himself. It was no exaggeration. The thin, pale little 5 foot 2½ inch Welshman, who never weighed more than 108 pounds, became the first flyweight champion of the world, and proved that his thin arms could also knock out bantams and featherweights.

Jimmy Wilde was born at Merthyr Tydfil, Wales, on 15 May 1892. At 14 he went into the coal mines, working in the smallest seams and developing great strength in his shoulders. After hundreds of fights in the popular booths of the day he turned professional when 18. Wilde won his first title in London four years later on 30 March 1914 when he knocked out Eugene Husson of France to become European flyweight champion. In the next six weeks, in Liverpool and London, he knocked out two more Frenchmen, Albert Bonzonnie and Georges Gloria, to retain the title. Next Jimmy faced Tancy Lee at London's National Sporting Club on 21 January 1915, with the vacant British title also at stake. The more experienced Lee cannily outboxed Jimmy, who had not quite shaken off an attack of flu, and stopped him in the seventeenth round.

On 14 February 1916 Wilde challenged Lee's conqueror, Joe Symonds, for what was billed as the British and world flyweight championship and stopped Symonds in the twelfth. Johnny Rosner, Tancy Lee and Johnny Hughes were all stopped in 1916, Wilde adding Lee's European title to his collection, and then Wilde fought Young Zulu Kid, an Italian who boxed out of Brooklyn and claimed the American championship. Some authorities cite this as the first true flyweight world championship bout. It was held on 18 December 1916 in London, with Wilde knocking out the Kid in the eleventh round.

Wilde's style was to hold his hands low, and to advance with his body swaying, ready to fire in shots from any angle. It was one of the styles Muhammad Ali adopted later. Pound for pound, Wilde could hit much harder than Ali. Of his 153 opponents, 101 were stopped. He was called the 'Mighty Atom,' or, because of his white, frail-looking body, the more imaginative 'Ghost with a Hammer in his Hand.'

During the First World War of 1914-18, Wilde was a sergeant instructor in the army, and unable to receive payment for fights. But one charity match at Chelsea Football Club's ground, Stamford Bridge, in which Jimmy stopped Joe Conn, a featherweight, resulted in a £3000 bag of diamonds for Mrs Wilde. Ironically, when Jimmy had married his Lisbeth as a teenager, one of her conditions had been that he should give up boxing. It was only the coincidence of a miner's strike and a forthcoming baby that had persuaded her later to soften her attitude. She became her husband's strongest supporter, accompanying him in training runs riding a bicycle.

Wilde dropped a rare decision to American bantam Pal Moore in 1918, but in 1919 triumphantly beat him and another American bantam, Joe Lynch, shortly to be champion of the world. In 1920 Wilde went to America, fighting the best, including the Zulu Kid, and registering five knockouts in an unbeaten 12 contests.

The beginning of the end came for Wilde in 1921, in an unfortunate manner. He agreed to fight American Pete Herman, the bantamweight champion, for the world title in London, despite giving away around 15 pounds. It was agreed in the contract that there should be a pre-fight weigh-in, to prevent Wilde having to give away too much weight. However, before leaving for England, Herman lost his crown to Joe Lynch (Wilde's victim of two years earlier) so the title was not at stake. That Herman

Below: Jimmy Wilde (left) boxing in 1919. The slim and frail-looking flyweight was nicknamed the 'Mighty Atom' and the 'Ghost with a Hammer in his Hand' for his furious punching. *Right:* Jimmy Wilde proudly wearing an original Lonsdale Belt. *Far right:* Wilde covers up in his bout in 1921 with the overweight bantam Pete Herman.

promptly regained the title on his return to the States was a little suspicious. More to the point, Herman refused to weigh-in, aware he was well overweight.

Wilde declined to fight, on the grounds that he was being tricked into giving away anything up to 25 pounds to an opponent who was four years younger and, moreover, a world champion. As the length of the hiatus increased, only the presence of the Prince of Wales calmed the increasingly irate fans, until Jimmy finally gave in, saying he would fight so as not to embarrass the Prince. The stronger Herman naturally wore Wilde down until the referee mercifully stopped it in the seventeenth.

Wilde, who had considered himself retired before fighting Herman, now retired officially. But two years later Tex Rickard offered him a big purse to go to America to defend the world flyweight title he had never lost against Pancho Villa, a fiery fighter from the Philippines. Against the advice of his wife, trainer and friends, the 31-year-old Wilde went. Although he lost he made many more American friends by the manner of his defeat, especially among the 23,000 who came to the Polo Grounds to see the contest. Wilde just would not give in, trying to fight back as Villa dealt out punishment for six rounds. Then, as the bell sounded to end the sixth and Wilde stopped boxing, a blow that the referee decided was already on its way knocked him clean out. Carried to his corner, he insisted on coming out dazed for the seventh, only to be knocked out again. He took hours to come round, and it was weeks before he recovered.

Shortly afterward Wilde retired, unable to avenge his last two defeats. He wrote a boxing column in a national newspaper for many years. The Ghost with a Hammer in his Hand died in Cardiff on 10 March 1969. He was the greatest of all the little men.

Benny Lynch
Tragic brilliance

Benny Lynch was one of the greatest flyweights, who had his hardest battle outside the ring. He had four world championship fights and won them all. His defeats came at the beginning of his short career, when he was learning, or at the end, when he was in a rapid decline. For about two years he boxed like a dream.

Lynch was born in the Gorbals, one of the poorest parts of Glasgow, Scotland, on 12 April 1913. His father encouraged him to box as an amateur, and as a teenager he gained much experience in the fairground boxing booths that travelled the country. As soon as he was 18 he turned professional. He was extremely busy and suffered a number of points defeats, four in 15 contests in 1931, three in 31 in 1932, one in 19 in 1933. That was the end of losing for a while. As his defeats got fewer, so his knockout victories increased. By 1934 he had developed into a superb, correct boxer, good defensively, clever in attack, and with a knockout punch in both hands.

He became Scottish flyweight champion, and in 1935 boxed Jackie Brown, the British and world champion, in a non-title bout at Glasgow. Brown was a seasoned campaigner and everybody was surprised when Lynch held him to a draw. Six months later, on 9 September 1935, Lynch went to Brown's home town of Manchester looking for the title, and knocked him down several times, forcing Brown to retire in the second round.

Among Lynch's 1936 contests was a brilliant defense against Pat Palmer, knocked out in the eighth round. On 19 January 1937 Small Montana (Philippines), who claimed the New York version of the title, was invited to London to attempt to win the more generally accepted version. Again it was a classic encounter, with both men demonstrating all the arts of boxing, but Lynch was given the well-deserved verdict.

On 13 October 1937, Lynch was challenged by the brilliant young apprentice blacksmith Peter Kane, of the large staring eyes, who, later on, was to be world champion for five years. Kane, from Golbourne, was only 19 and had little science, but he had tremendous stamina, displayed non-stop aggression and was in the habit of knocking out most of his opponents.

The contest was in Glasgow, where well over 30,000 packed Shawfield Park soccer ground to see it, and it was an outstanding battle. As they met in the middle of the ring at the start of round one Lynch caught Kane with a left-right combination that put the surprised young challenger down, and as the inexperienced Kane climbed to his feet too quickly Lynch moved in to finish it off. But a dazed Kane weathered the storm and then fought back so viciously in the second and third that Lynch was forced to revert to his boxing and forget a quick knockout.

As the fight progressed Lynch's more accurate punching gave him the initiative, but now and again Kane shook the champion with terrific punches that might have turned the tide. Eventually it was Lynch, however, who found the biggest punch, to put a tiring Kane down in the twelfth, and in the thirteenth the challenger was counted out draped over the bottom rope.

Lynch's delirious supporters little knew that they had seen their brilliant champion's last title defense. On 29 June 1938 Jackie Jurich (California) was the challenger but Lynch was 6½ pounds overweight and forfeited his crown. He knocked out Jurich in the catchweight contest which followed.

Lynch was now having great difficulty making the weight and was drinking hard in his frustration, which made it worse. He drew a return with Kane, but dropped four decisions against men not in his class. When he was knocked out, for the first time, by Aurel Toma of Romania in October 1938, he retired. He was only 25 but he was rapidly losing his battle with alcoholism. On 6 August 1946, still only 33 years old, he died. From brilliant world champion to complete physical wreck had taken about eight years.

Left: Benny Lynch (center) training outdoors for his title defense against Pat Palmer.

Above right: Benny Lynch puts Peter Kane on the canvas in their brilliant 1937 world title fight. All of Lynch's battles for the world crown were exciting contests, full of excellent boxing, and Benny won them all.

Below right: Lynch (right) boxing Aurel Toma of Romania in 1938. Lynch was only 25, but drink was destroying him, and he retired when Toma inflicted on him his first-ever knockout.

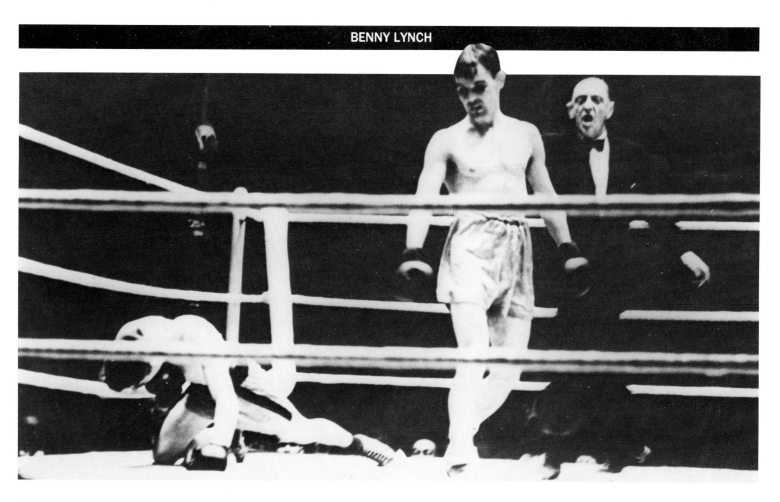

Pascual Perez
A fly with a kick

Pascual Perez was a boxing oddity among world champions. For a start he did not become a professional until he was 26 years old – an age by which a former flyweight king, Benny Lynch, had retired. Secondly, he was the first Argentinian to win a world title. Most amazing, perhaps, he was only 4 feet 11 inches tall and 105 pounds – the smallest man to win the world flyweight title.

Perez was born at Tupungato, Mendoza, Argentina, on 4 March 1926. He was one of nine children and the family was poor. He took up amateur boxing when he realized he had unusual strength and was so successful that he was selected for the Argentine team in the 1948 Olympics in London. Perez, who was well below the flyweight limit, was initially disqualified for being overweight, but it was an error – he had been confused with bantam teammate Arnoldo Pares. After that, Perez had no difficulty in winning the gold medal.

Back home, he was a clerk in the Chamber of Deputies in Buenos Aires, and his family urged him to give up boxing and work at this respectable job, but he continued to box under an assumed name. When he was found out he turned professional, but he was already well past 26

Above: The midget flyweight champion Pascual Perez chaired by his supporters after a 1955 defense in Tokyo against Yoshio Shirai, from whom he had taken the title six months earlier.

Left: Shirai goes down on one knee in the fight in which he lost the title to Perez, also in Tokyo. Shirai recovered, but Perez took the points decision.

Right: Pascual on the receiving end in his last title fight. In 1960 he tried to regain his crown from Thailand's Pone Kingpetch, but soon after taking this left in the eighth round he was stopped by the referee.

years old. He soon rattled up 50 victories, however, and in 1954 boxed a draw with world flyweight champion Yoshio Shirai in Buenos Aires. On 26 November 1954 he went to Tokyo and took the title with an emphatic points win, a victory he underlined six months later by knocking out Shirai in the fifth round in a fight which again took place before his Japanese supporters.

Perez was a terrific puncher, who stopped 56 of his 91 opponents, and often found his short stature an advantage as he bored in below the punches of taller opponents to blast them round the body.

In four years Perez disposed of 12 more challengers for his crown, seven inside the distance. Britain's Dai Dower failed by 12 seconds to last the first round, while three others went in three rounds each. He defended successfully in South America, the Philippines and Japan, but eventually dropped his title in Bangkok, Thailand. On 16 April 1960, Pone Kingpetch, ten years younger than the 34-year-old Perez, got a 15-round split decision, despite suffering a bad cut over his eye. On 22 September the two met again at Los Angeles, but the younger, aggressive Kingpetch stopped Perez in the eighth.

Pascual, who certainly loved his boxing, went on scrapping for four more years, but at 38 years old called it a day. In today's categories, he would probably be a light-flyweight, but for nearly six years the little man was king of the flyweights. Alas, this remarkable boxer was to die aged only 50 on 22 January 1977.

Index

Acknowledgments

The publisher would like to thank David Eldred who designed this book, Wendy Sacks the editor, Melanie Earnshaw the picture editor and Ron Watson who compiled the index. We would also like to thank the individuals and agencies listed below for supplying the pictures.
(T = top, B = bottom, L = left, R = right)

All-Sport: pages 1, 2 (all 3), 3 (L&R), 4, 5, 46 (T), 49 (all 3), 56, 57, 84 (T), 85 (T&B), 96 (T&B), 97 (T&B), 98 (B), 103 (B), 106, 107 (B), 109, 114, 115 (T&B).
Associated Press: pages 30 (B), 33, 42 (B), 46 (B), 48 (B), 50 (B), 51 (L), 53, 54, 65 (L&R), 72, 74 (T&BR), 76 (L), 78 (L), 82 (T&B), 83, 86 (R), 93 (B), 100, 104-5, 108, 110-11, 112 (R), 113, 118, 119, 127.
BBC Hulton Picture Library: pages 18, 19 (TR), 21 (L), 43, 50 (T), 51 (R), 60 (TR), 62 (L), 76 (R), 78 (R), 79 (B), 80 (R), 90-1, 94 (B).
BBC Hulton/Bettmann Archive: pages 8, 24 (T), 25 (T), 31 (B), 32, 34, 35 (BL), 41, 45, 55 (T&B), 63, 73 (BL), 87, 88-9, 95 (T), 116-17.
Boxing News: pages 10-11, 16 (T), 19 (L&BR), 20 (T), 21 (R), 22 (T&B), 23 (T&B), 24 (B), 25 (B), 26 (T&B), 27 (T&B), 28, 29 (T&B), 30 (T), 31 (T), 35 (TL), 36, 37 (L&R), 38 (T&B), 60 (BR), 61, 62 (R), 68, 69 (B&R), 71 (T&R), 75, 79 (L), 81, 90 (L), 91 (T&BR), 92 (T&B), 123 (L&R), 125 (T).
Joe Coughlan/Axis Agency: pages 16 (B), 52 (B), 60 (B).
Peter Newark's Western Americana: pages 12, 14-15, 15, 17 (L&R), 20 (T), 45 (R).
S&G Press Agency: pages 44 (T), 80 (L), 84 (B).
Frank Spooner Pictures: page 88 (L).
Bob Thomas Sports Photography: pages 99 (L), 103 (T).
TPS/Central Press: pages 39 (T&B), 40, 112 (L), 122, 125 (B), 126 (T&B).
TPS/Colour Library International: pages 9, 42 (T).
TPS/Fox: pages 120-1, 124.
TPS/Keystone: pages 35 (R), 44 (B), 47 (T), 48 (T), 52 (T), 66-7, 69 (TL), 70, 73 (T&R), 74 (BL), 77, 93 (T), 94 (T), 95 (B).